EARN EXTRA MONEY,

WORK AT YOUR

CONVENIENCE

YOUR GUIDE TO 21 REALISTIC INCOME OPPORTUNITIES WITH FLEXIBLE WORK SCHEDULES

M. Lashall Fitz

Earn Extra Money, Work at Your Convenience

Your Guide to 21 Realistic Part-time Income Opportunities with Flexible Work Schedules

Published by Betterment Books Publishing Company
ISBN 978-1482077612

First Edition, 2014
Printed in USA

Betterment Books Publishing Co.

Disclaimer

This book is designed to provide information about legitimate income part-time income opportunities only. This information is provided and sold with the knowledge that the publisher and author do not offer any legal or other professional advice. In the case of a need for any such expertise consult with the appropriate professional. This book does not contain all information available on the subject. This book has not been created to be specific to any individual's or organizations' situation or needs. Every effort has been made to make this book as accurate as possible. However, there may be information that might be dated. Therefore, this book should serve only as a general guide and not as the ultimate source of subject information. It is intended only to educate and inform. The author and publisher shall have no liability or responsibility to any person or entity regarding any loss or damage incurred, or alleged to have incurred, directly or indirectly, by the information contained in this book. You hereby agree to be bound by this disclaimer or you may return this book within the guarantee time period for a full refund.

Updated to
include 4 New
Bonus
Chapters!!

Introduction

The economy is changing; employers are cutting back and job security in not what it once was. Coupled with the high price of gas and the ever increasing cost of basic living expenses, many people are finding it hard to just make ends meet. Most people would love to have extra money coming in each month, but many don't have the desire or the time in their current lifestyle to take on a second job with set work hours in order to supplement their income.

If you are in need of a way to earn extra money to pay bills, buy gas, food, medication, fund your savings or just have extra spending money, then this book can help you. As you are about to learn, not only are there many ways to earn extra money without the exhaustion of working a traditional second job but these income opportunities will allow you the freedom to work when it's convenient for you.

Now not all of the opportunities listed in this book will be fitting for everyone. Some of the opportunities are tedious, some are fun, some can be boring and others don't pay as much money. Before starting, I suggest reading through the entire book to get a realistic understanding of each and every opportunity.

How to Use This Book

"Earn Extra Money, Work at Your Convenience" is divided into two sections:

SECTION ONE: Work "from" home opportunities. These are the opportunities that involve signing on with a company and performing most of the work outside of your home in various locations. Your home is used as your base to enter reports, your time, make calls, fax, etc.

SECTION TWO: Work "at" home opportunities. These are the opportunities that involve performing all of the work in your home.

What to Expect from This Book

I want to point out a few things about this book. As the title of this book indicates, the primary purpose of this book is to help you earn "extra" money. We've all seen the ads on the internet, "Make $87 an hour working part-time" or "Make fast cash working from home online", etc. Well this is definitely not that book!

You won't make $5,000 a month working part-time or earn money while you sleep. The income opportunities listed in this book are realistic. All of them can be easily started with no out of pocket costs. And don't worry none of them involve multi- level marketing, sales, chain letters, dog walking, plant watering or any other unrealistic, outdated or dumb ideas commonly found on the internet.

The second thing is most definitely don't expect a lot of pages full of boring information. (I hate reading those type books) I don't believe in wasting other people's time with useless information, especially when they are looking to learn something specific.

This book was designed to be a resource guide. What I have tried to do is keep the information concise and to the point. Some of the opportunities require more information and others do not, so you will find that some chapters are longer than others. My goal was to only include pertinent information that you would need about each opportunity.

So whether you need to make an extra $100 - $1,000 a month, you can be on your way to earning extra money, if you utilize the information in this book.

Okay, that's it. I'm done. I wish you much success in this and all your endeavors

Pay Scale Range Chart

Opportunity	Average Pay Rate (1hr/1 Assignment)	* Potential Monthly Earnings
Movie Checker	$12.00	$150-$300
Display Installer	$35.00	$150-$400
Field Inspector	$35.00	$700-$1,800
Drive By Inspector	$15.00	$800-$1,200
Field Interviewer	$11.00	$950-$1,800
Independent Field Agent	$15.00	$500-$800
Contract Driver	$35.00	$800-$2,000
Court Researcher	$10.00	$200-$500
Merchandiser	$12.00	$700-$1,800
Retail Data Collector	$10.00	$500-$900
Mystery Shopper	$12.00	$300- $400
Video Mystery Shopper	$50.00	$400-$1,500
Hospitality Evaluator	$35.00	$400-$700
Telephone Mystery Shopper	$5.00	$175-$400
At Home Freelance Agent	$15.00	$500-$2,000
Online Writer	$18.00	$600-$2,000
Virtual Assistant	$25.00	$500- $2,000

Online Tutor	$12.00	$500–$1,200
Micro Worker	$7.00	$300–$500
Website Tester	$10.00	$40–$200
Ads Search Quality Rater	$14.00	$900–$1,200
Data Entry	$10.00	$300–$400
Audio Transcriber	$12.00	$600–$1,500
Online Mock Juror	$25.00	$150–$400
Mail Decoy Agent	$20.00	$150–$400

*Figures intended only as a guideline.

WORK FROM HOME OPPORTUNITIES

In order to be successful, your desire for success *must* be greater than your fear of failure

READ THIS BEFORE YOU GET STARTED

#1.Many of the companies listed in this book pay via PayPal. If you do not have a PayPal account you can sign up for a free account at PayPal.com. It takes about 15 minutes to complete the process. Having a PayPal account is very helpful in other ways as well; you can use the account to shop online and as a way to safely send and receive money.

#2.Many of the companies that offer direct deposit are online companies. If you are uncomfortable using your personal bank account online, you can get a low or no fee prepaid debit American Express Serve, MasterCard or Visa card and use that instead. Many prepaid debit cards offer the same features that are standard in a regular bank account.

#3.The majority of the opportunities listed are independent contract opportunities. This just means you are paid by the job and not by the hour; taxes are not withheld from your pay and you are responsible for your own work. If you make over $600 a year as an independent contractor, the company will send you a 1099 at the end of the year. You will need to report the income when you file your income taxes.

On the good side, any and all of your direct out- of -pockets expenses incurred to complete the work, is fully deductible on your taxes.

Direct expenses can include:

- Gas
- Printing cost
- Furniture (chair, desk, lamp)
- Supplies (pens, paper, notebooks, etc.)
- Fees (internet, parking, registration, etc.)
- Cell Phone bill
- Equipment (camera, measuring tape, tools, printer, etc.)

To claim the deductions, you will need to keep a record of your expenses. For accurate recordkeeping, you can scan copies of your of receipts and save them to a file on your computer. Or use the old school method and keep all of your receipts in a shoebox.

If you set up a space in your home to use as a home office, a portion of your indirect costs can be deducted on you taxes as well.

Indirect expenses can include:

- Rent or mortgage payment
- Utility bill
- Property Insurance
- Maintenance costs

Indirect costs fall under Home Office Deductions. In order to claim these deductions, your work space has to be used regularly and exclusively to do your work. Even if you just use the space for doing research, filing reports or making calls, it qualifies as a home office.

To ensure you don't miss any deductions, you can get a copy of IRS Publication 587. (See your tax consultant for more help on this)

#4.Most of the independent contract opportunities will require you to provide your tax payer identification number and submit a W-9 form. If you are uncomfortable providing your social security online, you can always use an employer identification number (EIN) instead. If you don't have one, you can apply for one for free with the IRS.

1

Movie Checker

EMPLOYMENT STATUS Independent Contractor

EXPERIENCE REQUIRED None

OVERVIEW

Movie checkers are assigned to go to a chosen theatre to gather information about a particular movie. Sometimes referred to as Theatre Audits, this is an extremely easy but relatively unknown way to earn extra money.

If you are the type of person that enjoys the thrill of going to the movies, then you will love doing this type of work. The work is simple and straightforward.

Assignments can be either covert or overt. When you do a covert assignment, you are posing as a customer so you have to purchase a movie ticket. But you are reimbursed for the cost of the movie plus snacks.

You are not required to buy a ticket when completing overt assignments. But you must check in with theatre management before starting your assignment.

In most cases, you can't stay and watch the movie when you do overt assignments, unless you buy a ticket at your expense. Otherwise, you are required to leave the movie once you have completed your assignment. (*Unless the manager says it's okay for you to stay*)

Assignments can include performing:

- **Trailer Checks** - presenting a Letter of Authorization to the theatre manager to watch and record all trailers shown prior to an assigned feature.

- **Lobby Checks** - checking for promotional items throughout the theatre either openly or covertly, depending on the assignment.

- **Blind Checking -** covertly counting the number of movie goers (head count) for an assigned feature on an assigned day and or a particular show time. These assignments could also include checking the cleanliness of the lobby, restrooms, concession area and auditorium.

- **Open Checking -** presenting a Letter of Authorization to theatre management to count the number of movie goers attending the show time(s) of an assigned feature and collecting the box office information from management at the end of the day.

- **Theatre Evaluations -** posing as a movie goers and evaluating your experience as a customer. These assignments may include reporting how you were treated as a customer, the appearance and cleanliness of theatre, the appearance of staff and placement of marketing and/or promotional materials.

- **Sneak Preview Checking** - presenting a Letter of Authorization to theatre management to watch a sneak preview of an upcoming release, collecting the audience's reaction and demographic information.

- **All Screen Checking** – presenting a Letter of Authorization to theatre management to openly watch all the screens showing a particular feature and recording all the trailers and/or ads.

- **Advertisement Checks** - presenting a Letter of Authorization to openly watch and record all advertisements shown prior to an assigned feature(s).

- **Audience Reaction Checks** - openly or covertly attending an assigned feature and recording the audience's reaction.

- **Promotional Material Installations** - assembling movie standees, installing one-sheets (movie posters), banners, etc.

- **Exit Polling** - obtaining public opinion of a current movie

WORK SCHEDULE

Most assignments are performed on Fridays, Saturdays and/or Sundays. You have the option of choosing which assignments you want to complete, the theatre you want to visit and the day that's most convenient for you to work.

WHAT YOU CAN EXPECT TO EARN

Fees can range from $7 -$45. Some assignments pay a flat fee and others pay per task. The simplest assignments pay the lowest fees. It can take anywhere from 30 minutes to all day to complete an assignment.

PAY STRUCTURE

Most companies pay either once or twice a month and offer direct deposit or pay via PayPal.

DRAWBACKS

1.   Some assignments may require you to check the first showing on the first day of the movie opening.

2.   You won't be paid if you accept an assignment and the movie is not playing at the theatre as advertised.

3.   Opportunities can be limited if you don't live in or near a major city or if you live in a rural area.

4.   Assignments can be sporadic.

HYPOTHETICAL MOVIE CHECKER ASSIGNMENTS:

-You are assigned to do a trailer check. Your assignment is to watch the all of the opening trailers, record the number of trailers shown and make a note of the audience's response. You will only need to check one showing of the assigned movie. This assignment pays $12.00

-Your assignment is to do an open check and collect box office information (ticket sales) for an assigned movie. You will need to collect this information for all show times. The fee for this assignment is $45 for the first showing and $25 for each additional showing. So if the movie has 3 show times and is playing on two different screens, you would make $170

-You are assigned to put up a movie poster. This assignment pays $8.00

REQUIREMENTS TO GET STARTED

- ✓ At least 18 years old
- ✓ Have access to reliable transportation
- ✓ Have access to the internet
- ✓ An email address
- ✓ Have access to a scanner or fax to submit copies of paper report
- ✓ Have access to a digital camera or cell phone with a camera

FINDING OPPORTUNITIES

Companies generally post available assignments on their job boards or send out notifications via email. You can gain access to their job boards by registering for a **free** account.

TIME-SAVING/MONEY MAKING TIPS

1. Be sure to arrive fifteen to thirty minutes before the selected movie starts in the event of a long line. You don't want to risk not doing any parts of your assignment and not get paid for your time and effort.

2. Be sure to read the instructions carefully, you won't get paid if the assignment is not completed as instructed

3. Be sure to remember to have the manager sign off on your report before leaving the theatre when conducting overt assignments.

4. Be sure to register with several companies to increase your access to available jobs in your area

5. You can make more money if you accept last minute assignments. Some companies offer bonuses for completing last minute assignments.

KEYWORD SEARCH

For best search results, enter any of the following keywords

- Movie Theatre Checker
- Theatre Mystery Shopper
- Theatre Trailer Checker
- Movie Trailer Checker
- Movie Trailer Audit Jobs
- Movie Theatre Evaluator

Table 1-1 Movie Checker Opportunities

A Closer Look	a-closer-look.com
Bestmark	bestmark.com
Carol Media Services	carrollmedia.com
Checker Patrol	checkerpatrol.com
Confero	confero.com
Gigwalk	gigwalk.com
ICC/Decision Services	iccds.com
Imyst Inc.	imyst.com
MarketForce	marketforce.com
Michael & Associates	ishopforyou.com
MSP	mysteryshopperpros.com
National Shopping Services	nationalshoppingservices.com
Quality Assessments	qams.com
Rentrak	Ms.rentrak.com
Satisfaction Services Inc.	satisfactionservicesinc.com
Service Check	servicecheckreport.com
Service Sleuth	hsbrands.com
VeriTes	tnsmi-tes.com

2

Display Installer

EMPLOYMENT STATUS Independent Contractor

EXPERIENCE REQUIRED None

OVERVIEW

Display installers set up and install promotional and marketing displays in movie theatres, trade shows, retail stores or special events. This is a great way to earn extra money if you are mechanically inclined or enjoy putting things together. The work involves assembling a range of different types of displays that can include:

- Standees
- Posters
- Banners
- Point of purchase displays
- Special event display items

Most companies don't require any experience, you generally learn on the job. The work is not hard for the most part. Assembling some of the displays can be challenging, especially some of the large 3D theatre standee displays. Many of them, once assembled can be 10 feet high and 10 feet wide.

WORK SCHEDULE

You have the freedom to select only those projects that are of interest to you and fit within your schedule. Some assignment may require you to work on certain days or during certain hours. A typical assignment can take between 30 minutes to 3 hours to complete

Typical assignments can include:

- Assembling cardboard displays in local theaters (standees)
- Putting up promotional banners and/or posters
- Auditing current promotional material as needed.
- Miscellaneous theater display merchandising tasks

WHAT YOU CAN EXPECT TO EARN

Display installers are paid on a project basis. The average project pays between $25 and $35 per display.

PAY STRUCTURE

Most companies pay twice a month via and offer direct deposit.

DRAWBACKS

1. The work can be tedious and some of the more elaborate displays can be hard to assemble.

2. Not many companies offer this service.

3. Opportunities can be limited if you don't live in or near a major city or live in a rural area.

4. The work is not consistent; you may get 2-4 assignments 1 month and 10-12 assignments the next month.

REQUIREMENTS TO GET STARTED

- ✓ Be at least 18 years of age
- ✓ Have access to reliable transportation
- ✓ Be able to lift a minimum of 25 pounds
- ✓ Have the ability to take and email digital pictures of every installation
- ✓ Have an email address

FINDING OPPORTUNITIES

Most companies post available assignments on their job boards, contact you by phone or send out notifications via email. You can gain access to their job boards by registering for a **free** account.

Some companies run ads on the internet or on job boards such as Indeed.com, Careerbuilder.com or Simplyhired.com.

KEYWORD SEARCH

For best search results, enter any of the following keywords:

- Theatre Promotional Installs
- Theatre Display Merchandiser
- Theatre Display Installs
- Movie Standee Installer

Table 2-1 Display Installer Opportunities

Deluxe Media   deluxedisplays.net

MarketForce   marketforce.com

*VeriTes   tnsmi-tes.com

*May not have regular installment assignments

3

Freelance Field Inspector

EMPLOYMENT STATUS Independent Contractor

EXPERIENCE REQUIRED Little to None

OVERVIEW

Freelance field inspectors are independent contractors that perform field inspections for companies such as banks, mortgage companies, real estate agencies, credit unions, etc.

If you don't mind driving a lot, this can be a really good way to earn extra money and you have the potential to make a lot of money for doing really simple work.

The work involves performing basic inspections, collecting data and taking photos of the assigned property and/or business based on your instructions. The information you collect is reported on an inspection form and submitted online to the company requesting the inspection.

Field inspection is a broad field that includes many different types of inspections such as:

- Insurance Loss Inspections
- Occupancy Inspections
- Retail Outlet Verifications
- REO Inspections
- Sale Date Inspections
- Merchant Credit Card Site Inspections
- Drive By Inspections
- Bankruptcy Inspections

- Mortgage Inspections
- Vehicle Leasing Inspections
- Business Verifications
- FEMA Inspections

Believe it or not you don't need any prior experience, license or certification to get started as a Field Inspector. Some companies provide free training but most people learn on the job.

TIP

If you decide to pursue field inspection as a way to earn extra money, you will find that you will have more than enough work. There are many companies looking for honest and reliable people to conduct field inspections. Inspectors are needed in all zip codes across the country.

WORK SCHEDULE

You 're the boss; you set your own work hours and choose which assignments you want to accept, just as long as the inspections are completed by the due date.

Most field inspections need to be completed within 48 -72 hours, during the daylight hours and can be completed 7 days a week. You can work as much or as little as you want. The more you work the more you earn.

WHAT YOU CAN EXPECT TO EARN

Fees vary from industry to industry but can range from $7-$100 and up per assignment. The amount you are paid is based on the type of inspection. The average assignment takes 20 minutes to 1 hour to complete. Commercial inspections pay the highest fees, insurance in the middle and residential/ mortgage inspections pay the least

HYPOTHETICAL FIELD INSPECTION ASSIGNMENTS:

-You are assigned to do a Merchant Site Inspection. **Instructions**: you will need to contact the business to be inspected within 24 hours to schedule an appointment. When you meet with the contact, you will need to verify the physical address and take photos of the business license, exterior sign and file cabinet. This assignment pays $35.00

-You are assigned to do an Insurance Loss Inspection. **Instructions**: drive to the assigned residential address, verify the address and take 2 photos of damaged roof. This assignment pays $25

-You are assigned to do a Retail Outlet Verification. **Instructions**: you will need to visit the assigned business, verify the address and take a photo of the display of the requested product. This assignment pays $15.00

PAY STRUCTURE

The pay methods vary. Most companies pay via check. Some pay 10-15 days after the work is completed and others pay once a month or net 30.

DRAWBACKS

1.	Some opportunities may be hard to find because many field inspection companies don't advertise open jobs on job boards or in the classified section in the newspaper

2.	There are many national companies that try to take advantage of people new to the field by hiring them for low inspection fees. Many of these companies are connected with large, well-known banks and title companies.

3.	The work can put a lot of wear and tear on your car if you decide to work a lot.

4.	You will have a big tax bill at end of year if make a lot of money.

5.	Opportunities can be limited if you don't live in or near a major city or live in a rural area

REQUIREMENTS TO GET STARTED

- ✓ Have access to a computer with internet
- ✓ A Digital camera or cell phone that can take pictures
- ✓ Have access to reliable transportation
- ✓ An email address

FINDING OPPORTUNITIES

Some companies post available assignments on their websites, contact you by phone or send out notifications via email. You can gain access to their job boards by registering for a **free** account. Some companies may take a couple days to verify your social security number/EIN and/or conduct a background check.

You can find opportunities on:

- Craigslist in the job section listed under general labor or part-time jobs
- LinkedIn
- Job boards like: Monster, Simply Hired or Indeed.com

You can also find opportunities by:

1. Joining on SOFI.us. – Society of field inspectors a free membership website, that has a directory of companies that are hiring and other resources to get started.

2. Doing a keyword search online by state or zip

3. Contacting companies listed on Northamericanassociation.com- A free directory listing inspection companies

A WORD OF CAUTION

When searching online for opportunities:

- ✘ Be careful when answering ads advertising for "field reps needed asap" often times these are not actual job opening but affiliate ads looking to sell you an e-book.

- ✘ Beware of bank inspector job scams, these sites ask you to pay a fee for a starter kit and background check. You don't need a kit to get started as a field inspector.

TIME SAVING TIPS

Always do good work – If you take good pictures, fill out your forms correctly and complete your inspections on time, you will notice that the inspection company will consistently throw work your way.

Sign up with a lot of field inspection companies – Signing up with several different companies will give you access to more available assignments.

Don't take on more than you can handle – Reliable field inspectors get the best jobs, not overloading yourself will help you complete your assignments on time.

Work in several zip codes – The more zip codes you can work in, the more work you can get and the more money you can make. You never know, a zip code a few miles away just might be full of inspection jobs that pay higher fees.

Check your email often for available job notifications.

Consider getting trained as a FEMA inspector - FEMA uses field inspectors to assess property damages in the event of a natural disaster. This can be a great way to earn a lot of money in a short period of time

Perform a variety of inspections- Doing a variety of inspections will increase your chances to make more money and help keep the work interesting.

Never accept less than $10 per inspection – Unless you are doing a lot of small jobs in the same area or the job is on your route to work or home, anything under $10 wouldn't be worth your time and gas. (Especially since some companies can take up to 30 days to pay you).

KEYWORD SEARCH

For best search results, enter any of the following keywords:

- Field Inspector Jobs
- Field Inspection Companies
- Becoming a Field Inspector
- Field Inspectors Needed
- Independent Field Inspector
- Independent Field Agent
- Field Inspectors Wanted
- Field Service Inspectors

You can also search for opportunities in specific industries such as:

- Mortgage Field Inspectors
- Residential Field Inspectors

- Insurance Field Inspectors
- Property Field Inspectors

- Reo Inspections
- Insurance Loss Inspections

- Business Verification Inspections
- Merchant Site Inspections

- Foreclosure Field Inspectors
- Bank Field Inspectors

- Photo Inspections
- Occupation Inspections

Table 3-1 Field Inspection Opportunities

A1 Field Services
a1fieldservices.com

A2Z Field Services
a2zfieldservices.com

Aim Your Way
aimyourway.com

ASD America
asdamerica.com

CAC Services
go2cacs.com

Checkmate Inspections
checkmateinspections.com

CoreLogic
corelogic.com

Cyprexx
cyprexx.com

Douglas Guardian
douglasguardian.com

Facility Management Advisors
facilitymanagmentadvisors.com

Field Services, Inc.
fieldservices.com

Five Brothers Mortgage
fivebrms.com

ISN
isncorp.com

LPS Field Services
lpsfs.com

Madison Field Services, LLC
madisonfieldservices.net

Metro Inspections
metroinspections.com

Millennium Information Services
millinfo.com

National Creditors
nationalcreditors.com

National Field Representatives
nfronline.com

National Mortgage Field Services
nmfs.com

National Property Inspections
npiweb.com

Nationwide Field Inspections
nationwidefi.com

Nationwide Field Network
nationwidefieldnetwork.com

NEIS Inc.
neis1.com

GCS Field Research
gcsresearch.com

Guardian Portfolio Services
guardianps.com

Integrated Mortgage Solutions
imstoday.net

NVMS
nvms.com

PB Disaster Services
pbdisasterservices.com

Photoinspection.com
photoinspection.com

Property Transactor
propertytransactor.com

Quiktrak
quiktrak.com

Reliance Field Services
reliancefieldservices.com

REO Allegiance
1.reoallegiance.com

Research Specialist Inc.
rsireports.com

NIIS
nationalis.com

Northwest Loss Prevention
nwlpc.com

NRS
natrisk.com

Spectrum Field Services
spectrumfsi.com

Sprint Mortgage LLC
4smsi.com

TrendSource
trendsource.com

Trinity Real Estate Solutions
trinityonline.com

Universal Mortgage Field Services
universalmortgagfieldservces.com

Vectra Field Services
vectrafs.com

We Go Look
wegolook.com

4

Drive -By Inspector

EMPLOYMENT STATUS Independent Contractor

EXPERIENCE REQUIRED None

OVERVIEW

Drive-by inspectors are field inspectors that perform all of their inspections from the car. Drive-by inspections are quick assessments of a property. These inspections are done to assess both residential and commercial properties.

As you can guess, the work is really easy. It involves simply driving around your city or town, taking photos of the assigned properties, completing basic inspection forms and submitting the information online to the company requesting the inspection.

Information provided on these types of inspections can include:

- Multiple photos of the address and surrounding area
- Condition of property
- Verifying if the property is occupied

WORK SCHEDULE

Since you don't have to get out of the car, this one can easily be worked around your lifestyle. After you decide which assignments you want to work, just simply plan your route, get in your car and go to work.

WHAT YOU CAN EXPECT TO EARN

Fees for drive –by inspections vary by industry. The pay can range from $12 - $50 per assignment. Commercial assignments pay the highest fees. The average drive- by inspection takes 10-15 minutes to complete.

PAY STRUCTURE

See Chapter 3 - PAY STRUCTURE.

DRAWBACKS

See Chapter 3- Drawbacks

REQUIREMENTS TO GET STARTED

Valid driver's license

See Requirements to Get Started.

TIME-SAVING/MONEY MAKING TIPS

See Chapter 3- Time Saving-Money Making Tips

KEYWORD SEARCH

For best search results, enter any of the following keywords:

- Drive By Inspections
- Drive By Field Inspections
- Drive By Occupancy Inspections
- Drive By Inspection Jobs
- Drive By Surveys

- Drive By Mortgage Inspections
- Drive By Property Inspections
- Drive by Survey Inspection
- Drive By Inspection Companies
- Drive By Bank Inspections

Table 4 -1 Drive- By Inspection Opportunities

Aim Your Way
aimyourway.com

National Field
Representatives
nfronline.com

Central Valley Field Services
centralvalleyfieldservices.com

National Mortgage Field
Svcs *nmfs.com*

CWIS LLC
cwis-llc.com

Nationwide Field Services
nationwidefieldservices.com

Facility Management Advisors
facilitymanagmentadvisors.com

NRS
natrisk.com

Field Inspectors LLC
aefieldinspectors.com

Photoinspection.com
photoinspection.com

Field Services Inc.
fieldservices.com

Sentinel
sfsco.net

JMI Reports
jmireports.com

Sprint Mortgage LLC
4smsi.com

LPS Field Services
lpsfs.com

TrendSource
trendsource.com

Metro Inspections
metroinspections.com

Trinity Real Estate Solutions
trinityonline.com

Mortgage Field Inspections
msmortgagefieldinspections.web.com

We Go Look
wegolook.com

5

Field Interviewer

EMPLOYMENT STATUS W2

EXPERIENCE REQUIRED Prior Interviewing or Similar Work Experience

OVERVIEW

Field Interviewers conduct face-to face interviews with selected participants on research projects. The work involves contacting respondents at their homes, businesses, or schools to conduct the interviews.

The interviews are conducted using a laptop or paper questionnaire, depending on the requirements of the research project. Once the information is collected, it is transmitted back to the home office.

The work can be really interesting. The research projects often obtain information on issues such healthcare, employment, family life, education, etc.

This is a good way to earn extra money if you enjoy meeting and interacting with new people from all walks of life; hearing other people's point of view. Some companies require prior field interviewing experience and others accept similar work/life experience.

WORK SCHEDULE

You have the freedom to set your own work schedule just as long as the schedule meets the demands of the research project. Interviews are generally conducted in the evening and/or on the weekends or whenever participants are available.

WHAT YOU CAN EXPECT TO EARN

The average starting pay is generally between $11.00and $13.00 per hour. Most companies pay for your drive time and reimburse for mileage, meals and lodging if you are required to travel for a project.

PAY STRUCTURE

Pay dates and methods vary. Most companies pay twice a month and offer direct deposit.

DRAWBACKS

1. The work can be tiring, and stressful

2. You are required to complete the assigned project regardless of weather conditions.

3. Some participants can be difficult and uncooperative.

4. Projects may require you to work in a bad neighborhood.

5. There can be big gaps between research projects.

REQUIREMENTS TO GET STARTED

- ✓ A valid driver's license
- ✓ Proof of car insurance
- ✓ Access to reliable transportation
- ✓ Familiar and comfortable using a laptop computer

FINDING OPPORTUNITIES

Most companies run ads on the internet, on job boards such as Indeed.com, Careerbuilder.com or Simplyhired.com or post opening on their websites.

You can also find additional opportunities on:

- Craigslist (generally listed under part-time jobs or ETC)
- College Websites-Research Department
- Survey Research Centers
- US Government Sites
- Part-time job boards
- Newspaper classified ads (online and print)
- LinkedIn

KEYWORD SEARCH

For best search results, enter any of the following keywords:

- Field Data Collector jobs
- Part-time Field Interviewer jobs
- Survey Research Centers
- Field Data Collection companies
- Part-time Research Field Interviewer

Table 5-1 Field Interviewer Opportunities

NHSDA (SAMSHA)	nsduhweb.rti.org
Nielson Company	nielson.com
NORC	norc.org
Mathematica Policy Research	mathematica-mpr.com
RTI International	rti.org
Westat	westat.com

6

Independent Field Auditor

EMPLOYMENT STATUS Independent Contractor

EXPERIENCE REQUIRED None

OVERVIEW

Independent field auditors are independent contractors that perform a variety of retail, compliance and procedural audits. These services are provided by a variety of companies including mystery shopping and merchandising companies.

The work is generally fairly simple. It involves visiting an assigned business, performing services based on the instructions and completing a report form. The form is submitted online directly to the company's website.

Work can include:

- Product Recalls
- Retail Quality Audits
- Product Retrievals
- Consumer Complaint Retrievals
- On-site validations
- Compliance evaluations
- Physical inventory

WORK SCHEDULE

You have the freedom to select only the assignments you want to complete. Once you accept an assignment, it must be completed within the specified time frame. You can work as little or as much as you want.

WHAT YOU CAN EXPECT TO EARN

Fees vary. Rates are paid based on the nature of the assignment. Fees can be as low as $3 per task and up to $150 per assignment. Assignments can take anywhere from 10 minutes up to three hours to complete.

PAY STRUCTURE

Pay dates and methods vary. Most companies pay twice a month and offer direct deposit.

DRAWBACKS

1. The work flow can be inconsistent.
2. Some of the fees for assignments can be low and not worth your time.

REQUIREMENTS TO GET STARTED

- ✓ An email address
- ✓ Access to reliable transportation
- ✓ Access to internet
- ✓ Scanner or fax
- ✓ Cell phone that can take pictures

FINDING OPPORTUNITIES

Companies generally post available assignments on their job boards or send out notifications via email. You can gain access to their job boards by registering for a **free** account.

KEYWORD SEARCH

For best search results, enter any of the following keywords:

- Quality Assurance Auditor
- Independent Contractor Retail Audits
- Independent Auditor Jobs
- Independent Field Agent

Table 6-1 Field Auditor Opportunities

Ardent Services Inc.	ardentservices.com
Clicknwork	Clicknwork.com
Field Agent	fieldagent.net
GCS Research	gcsresearch.com
Goodwin Hospitality	mysteryshopperprogram.com
LRA Worldwide	lraworldwide.com
RQA Inc.	rqa-inc.com

Sinclair Customer Metrics	sinclaircustomermetrics.com
Spar Business Services	sparinc.com
Stericycle	stericycle.com
Trend Source	trendsource.com
We Go Look	wegolook.com

7

Contract Driver (Car)

EMPLOYMENT STATUS Independent Contractor

EXPERIENCE REQUIRED None

OVERVIEW

Contract Drivers are Independent contractors that are paid to drive their personal vehicle. This is one of the more lucrative ways to earn extra money. The work is easy and straight forward

It can involve:

- Delivering packages
- Ride sharing
- Carpooling
- Providing Private Transportation
- Route deliveries

WORK SCHEDULE

You have complete freedom to create your work schedule and pick the assignments you want to complete. You determine how little or how much you want to work and earn.

WHAT YOU CAN EXPECT TO EARN

The average fee is around $30-$35 per hour.

PAY STRUCTURE

Most companies pay weekly and offer direct deposit.

DRAWBACKS

1. The work can put a lot of wear and tear on your car.
2. Opportunities may not be available in all areas.

REQUIREMENTS TO GET STARTED

✓ Must be at 21 years old
✓ Have a valid driver's license
✓ Pass a background check
✓ A smart phone

FINDING OPPORTUNITIES

Most companies post job openings on their websites. Many, if not all of them run ads online.

KEYWORD SEARCH

For best search results, enter any of the following keywords:

- Independent Contract Drivers
- Ridesharing Companies
- Ridesharing Driver Jobs
- Delivery Contract Driver Jobs

Table 7-1 Contract Driver Opportunities

Courier Express	courierexpress.net
Lyft	lyft.com
RideJoy	ridejoy.com
RideShare	rideshare.com
Uber	uber.com

8

Court Researcher

EMPLOYMENT STATUS Independent Contractor

EXPERIENCE REQUIRED Some/Some Companies offer free training

OVERVIEW

Court researchers perform research of various court documents from available public records. The type of research that is conducted done is dependent upon the needs of the client.

The work is quite simple. It generally involves retrieving the requested information from the court records needed by the client and entering the information into a database or spreadsheet software.

Assignments vary but can involve researching:

- Mortgage records
- Judgments
- Tax liens
- Marriages
- Bankruptcies
- Foreclosures
- Probates

Some companies prefer to hire only experience court researchers. Companies that hire inexperienced researchers generally offer free training

WORK SCHEDULE

There are no set work hours. You have the flexibility to collect records anytime during court house hours.

WHAT YOU CAN EXPECT TO EARN

The average researcher earns $10-$15 per hour. Experienced researchers earn $25 per hour and up.

PAY STRUCTURE

Pay dates and methods of pay vary. Most companies offer direct deposit and pay once or twice a month.

DRAWBACKS

1. There may not be many open opportunities in certain cities
2. Opportunities may be limited if you live in rural area
3. The work can be inconsistent
4. You won't get paid for your mileage or drive time to and from the courthouse

REQUIREMENTS TO GET STARTED

- ✓ Access to computer with internet
- ✓ An email address
- ✓ Access to reliable transportation
- ✓ A cell phone
- ✓ Ability to type

FINDING OPPORTUNITIES

Most companies post job openings on their websites. Many run ads online

A WORD OF CAUTION

Watch out for sites that charge a fee for starter kits or certifications. You don't need a starter kit or a certificate to become a court researcher.

KEYWORD SEARCH

For best search results, enter any of the following keywords:

- Court Researcher Jobs
- Court Researchers Wanted
- Independent Court Researcher
- Courthouse Researchers
- Court Researching Companies
- Court Records Researchers
- Court Researchers Needed
- Become a Court Researcher
- Court Researcher Work from Home

Table 8-1 Court Researcher Opportunities

Accurate Background   accuratebackground.com

Advantage Background Check   abcheck.com

Background Profiles   backgroundprofiles.com

Castle Branch   castlebranch.com

Court Couriers   courtcouriers.com

Deed Collector   deedcollector.com

First National Acceptance Co.   financusa.com

Harvey E Morse, P.A.   findanheir.com

Hire Right   hireright.com

Information Direct   informationdirect.us

Information Technologies Inc.   inft.net

IT-Boss Research   itbossresearch.com

Jelly Bean Services   work4jbs.com

Lighthouse Information Services   lighthouseinfoserv.com

Mail Co Productions   mailcoproductions.com

Mid-South Information Services   midsouthinfo.com

Omni Data Retrieval   omnidataretrieval.com

Sentinel Screening Inc.   sentinelscreening.com

Tax Sale Lists	taxsalelists.com
The Screening Group	thescreeninggroup.com
Validity Screening Solutions	validityscreening.com
Wholesale Screening Solutions	wholescreening.com
Wolfgang Research	wolfgangresearch.com

9

Merchandiser

EMPLOYMENT STATUS Independent Contractor/W2

EXPERIENCE REQUIRED Little to None

OVERVIEW

Merchandisers are 3rd party vendors hired by merchandising companies to perform varies retail tasks. Assignments can range from on-going part -time assignments, short term projects, route work, week end only projects or temporary special projects. Some assignments can also include you working on a team and/or traveling to other cities.

Merchandisers most often work in major retail outlets such as, Walmart, Kroger, Dollar General, Home Depot, etc.

Tasks can include:

- Delivering new stock
- Offering product samples to customers
- Rotating stock
- Installing promotional signs
- Ensuring that the merchandise is displayed correctly
- Ensuring that the proper level of stock is maintained
- Taking Inventory and Performing Audits
- Setting up, tearing down or re-setting displays and /or promotional shelves
- Conducting physical product recalls

The experience required to become a part time merchandiser varies. Companies that hire independent contractors generally don't require any type of experience.

For a number of different reasons, some companies that hire W-2 employees prefer to hire people that have some sort of merchandising experience. But if you have worked in any type of retail environment, this experience usually is enough to get your foot in the door with some companies.

WORK SCHEDULE

Merchandisers enjoy the benefit of having a steady paycheck and working flexible hours. Some companies use self-scheduling software, which gives you the ability to choose the assignments you want to complete. Other companies assign work assignments by territory.

Some assignments may require you to work on certain days or only during certain hours. But for the most part you can visit your assigned stores on the days and during the times that are most convenient for you.

WHAT YOU CAN EXPECT TO EARN

The amount you can expect to earn depends on your employment status. Independent contractors are paid per task. Fees can range from $10.00 - $25.00 per task. The pay for W-2 employees can range from $8.50 - $15.00 per hour. Companies that hire merchandisers as W-2 employees, generally pay for gas mileage, training and have some sort of bonus program.

Part-time merchandisers that work for one company, earn on average $600 - $1,200 a month. You can expect to earn more if you work as an independent contractor and/or part time employee or work for more than one company.

PAY STRUCTURE

Most companies that hire W-2 employees pay weekly or bi-monthly. The majority of companies that hire independent contractors pay once a month; a few pay twice a month. Most all of the companies offer an option for direct deposit or pay via check.

DRAWBACKS

1. Some work projects can be tedious
2. The pay for some jobs can be too low for the amount of work required
3. Some merchandising companies can have unreasonable deadlines.
4. The work flow for some companies that hire independent contractors can be inconsistent.
5. Pay raises can be slow for merchandisers that are W-2 employees

REQUIREMENTS TO GET STARTED

✓ Have an email address
✓ Physically able to lift at least 25 pounds
✓ Understand basic merchandising terms
✓ Ability to read plan-o-gram
✓ Access to reliable transportation
✓ Ability to take product inventory

FINDING OPPORTUNITIES

Most companies post job openings on their websites. Many, if not all of them run ads online or post openings on job boards such as Indeed.com, Careerbuilder.com or Simplyhired.com.

Some companies post ads on Craigslist for special projects. The ads are generally listed in the job section under retail, general labor or part-time job.

You can also find opportunities on the following merchandising resource websites:

Volition.com
MrCheckout.net

TIME-SAVING/MONEY MAKING TIPS

The easiest way to get started as a merchandiser is to start with one or more of the companies that hire independent contractors. These jobs are usually very easy to get. The work can be sporadic with some companies but this will give you a basic understanding of the field of merchandising and it's a good way to earn while you learn.

KEYWORD SEARCH

For best search results, enter any of the following keywords:

- Part-time Merchandisers
- Retail Merchandiser Jobs
- Merchandising Jobs
- Part-time Field Merchandiser Jobs
- Merchandising Companies
- Independent Reset Merchandiser Jobs

Table 9-1 Merchandiser Opportunities

Acosta	acosta.com
ASC Retail Merchandising	ascretail.com
Action Link	actionlink.com
Advantage Sales & Marketing	asmnet.com
Aisle One Merchandising	aisleonemerchandising.com
American Greetings	corporate.americangreetings.com
AMS Retail Solution	merchandiser.net
Anderson Merchandisers	amerch.com
Apollo Retail	apolloretail.com
Ardent Services Inc.	ardentservices.com
*At Your Service	aysm.com
ATA Retail Services	ataretail.com
BDS Marketing	bdsmarketing.com
*Castforce	castforce.net
Channel Partners	channelpartners.com
Chuck Latham	clareps.com
Convergence Marketing	convergencemktg.com

CPM	us.cpm-int.com
Crossmark	crossmark.com
Demo Sales Inc.	demosales.net
Driveline Retail	drivelineretail.com
DSI	distributionservices.com
Foot Print Retail	prismretail.com
Hallmark Cards	hallmark.com
HDA Merchandising	hdamerchandising.com
*ICC/ Decision Services	iccds.com
Lawrence Merchandising	lmsvc.com
MarketStar	marketstar.com
Merchandise Management Co.	merchmanco.com
Mosaic Jobs	mosaicjobs.com
National Merchandising	natlm.com
News America Marketing	newsamerica.com
Premium Retail Services	wearepremium.com
*Quest Service Group	questservicegroup.com
Readerlink	readerlink.com
Revenue Creations	revenuecreations.com

RMS	rmservicing.com
SAS Retail Services	sasretailservices.com
Set & Service Resources	sasrlink.com
Shelf Tech	shelftech.com
*Spar Group	sparinc.com
USA Merchandising Solutions	usamerchandising.com
WIS International	w3.wisintl.com
Wolf Retail Services	wolfretail.com
Work Smart Merchandising	wsmerchandising.com

*Indicates companies that hire independent contractors

10

Retail Data Collector

EMPLOYMENT STATUS W2

EXPERIENCE REQUIRED None

OVERVIEW

Retail data collectors collect consumer retail data from a variety of retail stores. This data is collected by scanning the UPC codes on products. This is another really easy way to earn extra money.

The work is a no brainer. It involves you going to a selected store and scanning the bar code labels located on ads, promotional items, store displays and/or store shelving.

Duties can include:

- Reconciling purchase invoices against inventories
- Scanning UPC codes via hand-held device
- Collecting display and promotional information
- Inputting product price information
- Collecting and entering custom survey data
- Transmitting collected data via internet

Most companies don't require any experience. As long as you have the time, can do the work and meet the basic requirements.

WORK SCHEDULE

Retail data collectors have the flexibility to set their own work schedules. Since the data is collected primarily from retail stores that are open late 7 days a week, you can collect data at 10pm if you like or 3 am if the store is open 24 hours. It doesn't matter, as long as the projects are completed by the due dates.

HOW MUCH YOU CAN EXPECT TO EARN

The pay range is generally between $8.50 and $12.00 per hour. Most companies pay for drive time and mileage. The work hours range from 5-20 hours a week depending on the project.

PAY STRUCTURE

Most companies offer direct deposit and pay twice a month.

DRAWBACKS

1. There are not many companies that offer this service
2. Opportunities can be limited if you live in a rural area

REQUIREMENTS TO GET STARTED

- ✓ Valid driver's license
- ✓ Access to reliable transportation
- ✓ Proof of car insurance
- ✓ Ability to lift up to 25 lbs. and stand for up to 5 hours
- ✓ Ability to travel within a 60 mile radius from home

FINDING OPPORTUNITIES

Most companies post job openings on their websites. Many, if not all of them run ads online or on job boards such as Indeed.com, Careerbuilder.com or Simplyhired.com

KEYWORD SEARCH

For best search results, enter any of the following keywords:

- Retail Data Collector Jobs
- Retail Data Collection Companies
- Retail Merchandiser Surveyor

Table 10-1 Retail Data Collector Opportunities

Crossmark	crossmark.com
Retail Data	retaildatallc.com
RGIS	rgis.com
SAS Retail	sasretailservices.com

NOTES

11

Mystery Shopper

EMPLOYMENT STATUS Independent Contractor

EXPERIENCE REQUIRED None

OVERVIEW

Mystery shoppers (*also called secret shoppers)* are undercover customers who visit businesses posing as customers. Contrary to many of the ads you may have seen on the internet, mystery shoppers are actually paid to gather information and not to shop per se.

The work is very simple. It involves visiting an assigned business and evaluating the service(s) based on your instructions. The information you collect is reported on an evaluation form that is submitted online to the mystery shopping company

Mystery shopping is one the easiest ways to earn extra money. It's unique, fun and can be very interesting. The Mystery shopping industry is huge. There are literally hundreds of mystery shopping companies in the United States, so you can always find work.

Anyone over the age of 18 can become a mystery shopper. You don't need any experience, special skills or equipment to do the work. You just need to meet the basic requirements

Mystery shops are conducted in all types of industries:

- Retail Shops
- Restaurants
- Storage Facilities
- Airports

- Banks
- Hotels
- Gas Stations
- Tanning Salons

- Apartment Complexes
- Dealerships
- Entertainment venues
- Service facilities

WORK SCHEDULE

One of the greatest benefits of mystery shopping is that the work is extremely easy to incorporate it into your lifestyle. Most companies use self – scheduling software systems. This simply means you have the option of choosing which assignments you want to complete. Once you accept an assignment, you have the flexibility to complete the assignment on your own schedule just as long as it's done and reported by the due date.

You can choose assignments that will allow you to work one Saturday a month, two days a week or ten times a month. Or if you want to make a steady income, you can choose to work a lot of assignment throughout the week. It's completely up to you

Typical assignments can include:

- Checking the cleanliness of the store
- Evaluating employee(s) customer service skills
- Checking the quality of a product
- Checking to see if a particular product is displayed correctly
- Checking signage(s)

- Buying an particular item or service
- Inquiring about a certain product or service

WHAT YOU CAN EXPECT TO EARN

The fee you are paid as a shopper is based on the amount of time needed to complete the assignment and the report. The fee can range from $12-$25 for simple assignments and $40- $250 for more complex assignments.

Big tickets assignments like home, cars and bank mystery shops often pay higher fees. Normal assignments take anywhere from 15 minutes to an hour to complete.

Some assignments may require you to purchase an item or pay for a service. In that case, you are reimbursed and you get to keep the merchandise. Assignments that are more complex or require that you drive a longer distance from your home usually pay higher fees or include a bonus.

PAY STRUCTURE

There are a small number of companies that only pay via check. But most companies offer direct deposit or pay via PayPal

Pay dates vary. The majority of companies pay once a month. There are a few that pay twice a month. A very slim few pay weekly. Before registering with a mystery shopping company, you can find this information in their FAQ

DRAWBACKS

1. Although, Mystery shopping is an easy way to earn extra money, it would take a lot of effort to earn more than $500 a month. You can make up to $300-$400 a month very easily by doing 10-14 shops a month without interrupting your current lifestyle. To make more than that, you would really need to get your hustle on.

2. Unlike starting a traditional part-time job, you won't generate a regular income right away mystery shopping. All mysteries shopping companies are not alike. Some have regular assignments and others are more sporadic. Some companies only do work in certain industries (groceries, retail, restaurants, etc.) and there are some that do work in all types of sectors.

It takes a couple of months, to learn which companies offer regular assignments and to build up your reputation as a shopper to get access to more assignments

3. Some companies pay slowly. They may only pay once a month and only pay by check. Some can take as long as 45 days to pay you.

REQUIREMENTS TO GET STARTED

- ✓ Have access to the internet
- ✓ An email address
- ✓ Have access to transportation
- ✓ Have access to a scanner or fax to submit copies of paper reports (Figure 11-1)
- ✓ Have access to a digital camera or cell phone with a camera

Hypothetical Mystery Shopping Assignments:

- Your assignment is to pose as a potential customer at a car dealership to evaluate the service you receive. You will be required to take a test drive. This assignment could take approximately 40 to 90 minutes to complete. It pays $50.00

- Your assignment it to go to Regions Bank and inquire about their mortgage products to evaluate how much information the sales associate knows about the products. This assignment could take approximately 35 to 45 minutes to complete. The bank is located 25 miles from your home. It pays $75.00 plus a $15.00 bonus.

- Your assignment it to purchase groceries from Kroger to evaluate the cleanliness of the bathroom, your wait time in line and report if the cashier greeted you. You will be reimbursed for your groceries up to $20.00. This assignment could take 15 to 30 minutes to complete. It pays $18.00

FINDING OPPORTUNITIES

Most companies post available assignments on their job boards or send out notifications via email. You can gain access to their job boards by registering for a **free** account

In some cases, you may gain immediate access to the job board and actually get an assignment the same day. Most companies take a couple days to verify your social security number or EIN.

HERE'S HOW THE COMPLETE PROCESS WORKS:

Step 1 You register online at the mystery shopping company's website to become a shopper

Step 2 Once you are approved to become a shopper, the Mystery shopping company will set up an account for you in their portal and email you your login information.

Step 3 You log onto the portal to update your profile by entering your demographic information, the zip codes or cities you prefer to work in and the way you want to receive your pay (i.e. PayPal, check).

Step 4 That's it. You use the portal to search
for available assignments, enter your reports and track payments

You can also find opportunities by:

1. Signing up with several mystery shopping scheduling services (Table 11-2). Scheduling services schedule assignments for many different shopping companies.

2. Submitting an application to be a shopper on Archon Development website, archondev.com. Archon is a scheduling system that will automatically distribute your contact information to its affiliated mystery shopping companies.

3. Signing up for a free account with any or/all of the following job boards:

a. JobSlinger - JobSlinger.com

b. MSJobBoard - MSJobBoard.com

c. Mystery Shopping Solutions- Mystshopsol.com

d. Mystery Shop Forum – Mysteryshopforum.com

A few companies run ads on the internet or on job boards such as Indeed.com, Careerbuilder.com or Simplyhired.com

TIP

There are many people earning a living working as professional mystery shoppers. If you find that you really like mystery shopping and want to become a Certified Professional Shoppers, you can find more information online by visiting the Mystery Shopper Providers Association website: mysteryshop.org/certification.

A WORD OF CAUTION

Unfortunately, the Mystery shopping industry has been plagued by scammers. To protect yourself, stick with company websites that are associated with the Mystery Shoppers Providers Association (MSPA), certified by the Better Business Bureau or are well known companies.

Don't do business with any company that:

- ✖ Requires you to pay a fee for certification in order to accept assignments
- ✖ Charges a fee to access "hidden" mystery shopping opportunities
- ✖ Sell directories of companies that hire mystery shopping companies
- ✖ Solicit you without permission via email
- ✖ Ask you to deposit a check and then wire some of the money back to them

Real mystery shopping companies don't charge any fees to get started or to access their job boards. If you have an encounter with a mystery shopping scam, you can file a complaint with the FTC, your State Attorney General or the Better Business Bureau.

TIME-SAVING/MONEY MAKING TIPS

Read the guidelines and instructions very carefully before accepting an assignment. Only accept assignments that you are comfortable performing. Not following instructions can result in getting fewer assignments. You won't get paid if an assignment is not completed according to the guidelines. In almost all cases, you will be required to re-do the assignment at your expense.

Make sure the fee that is offered is worth your time and gas. You don't want to take an assignment that pays less than $25.00 if you have to drive more than 20 miles back and forth to complete the assignment

Complete assignments on time. Completing assignments on time is very important in the Mystery shopping industry. Not completing assignments can also decrease your ranking which can affect your chances of getting future assignments. If you find you can't complete the assignment on times, its' best to email the scheduler to get the due date extended

Register with several different Mystery Shopping companies, scheduling services and Mystery Shopping job boards. Because there is no way of predicting which companies will have assignments in your area, this will increase your access to more available job assignments

Don't always take the first fee that is offered to complete an assignment. Sometimes, the first fee offered is not the most the mystery company is willing to pay to get the job done. In some cases, it pays to wait it out before taking an assignment- some assignments have rigid deadlines so the longer an assignment sits on the job board, the higher the fee goes up. Of course, there's always the chance that another shopper will grab the job once the fee goes up which brings us to the next tip.

Set up an email address just for mystery shopping. Mystery shopping jobs are offered on a first-come, first-serve basis. Once the good assignments become available, they are grabbed up quickly. You can elect to be notified by email when new assignments come available. Setting up a separate email account will help you stay organized and not miss any new opportunities and/or the higher paying assignments.

Watch the job boards. If you want to increase your chances of getting more assignments and keep watch of when the fees are increased or a bonus is added to an assignment, then it's best to check the job boards as often as you can throughout the day. As a rule of thumb, you may want to get in the habit of checking the board(s) when you are online checking your email or social media accounts

Incorporate Mystery shopping into your lifestyle. You may possibly find assignments that you can complete on your way to work, school, the doctor's office, the grocery store, running errands, etc. Many mystery shopping companies have available assignments all over the country. You can search for assignments when you go on vacation or out of town to visit relatives. You could possibly make enough to supplement or even pay for the trip

Accept last minute assignments. For one reason or another, some shoppers don't' complete their assignments. Very often this happens at the last minute. This of course, puts the mystery shopping company in a bind. You benefit because last minutes assignments often include a bonus

KEYWORD SEARCH

For best search results, enter any of the following keywords:

- Mystery Shoppers
- Mystery Shopper Jobs
- Secret Shopper
- Retail Secret Shopper
- Mystery Shopping Companies
- Mystery Shopping Scheduler Jobs

You can also search for opportunities in specific industries such as:

- Restaurant Mystery Shopping
- Apartment Mystery Shopping
- Automotive Mystery Shopping

Table 11-1 Mystery Shopper Opportunities

A Closer Look
a-closer-look.com

Creative Image
creativeimage.net

About Face
aboutfacecorp.com

Customer Impact
customerimpactinfo.com

Amusement Advantage
amusementadvantage.com

Customer Service Experts
customerserviceexperts.com

Ann Michaels & Associates
ishopforyou.com

Customer Perspectives
customerperspectives.com

Asset Protection Associates
assetprotectionassociates.net

Data Quest Ltd
dataquestonline.com

Assurance Performance
apartmysteryshoppers.com

DSG Associates
dsgai.com

At Your Service
aysm.com

Ellis Mystery Shoppers
ellismysteryshopperjobs.com

Baird Consulting Group
barid-group.com

Feedback Plus Inc.
feedbackplus.com

Bare International
bareinternational.com

Gap Buster
gapbuster.com

BDS Marketing Inc.
bdsmktg.com

GFK Mystery Shopper
cybershoppersonline.com

Beyond Hello Inc.
beyondhello.com

Goodwin Hospitality Shopper
mysteryshopperprogram.com

Brandt Group
thebrandtgroup.com

Cirrus
cirrusmktg.com

Confero
conferoinc.com

Count On Us
ucountonus.com

Informa Research
informars.com

Insula Research
insulareserch.com

I-Spy Hospitality Audit Svc
ispy4u.net

Integrity Consultants
integrityconsultants.us

Intelli-Shop
intelli-shop.com

Interaction Mystery Shop
interactionsmarketing.com

Jancyn
jancyn.com

Management Consulting
Group
managementconsultingroup.com

HS Brands International
hsbrands.com

ICC/Decision Services
iccds.com

ICU Associates
icuassociates.com

Imyst
imyst.com

Mystery Inquiries, Inc.
mysteryinquiries.com

Mystery Researchers
mysteryresearchers.com

Mystery Shopper Services
mysteryshopperservices.com

Mystique Shopper
mystiqueshopper.com

National Shopping Service
nationalshoppingservice.com

New Image Mktg. Research
nimltd.com

Nsite
nsiteinc.com

NW Loss Prevention Group
nwlpc.com

Maritz Research
maritzmysteryshopping.com

Market Endeavors
marketendeaveors.biz

Market Force International
marketforce.com

Market ViewPoint
marketviewpoint.com

Marketwise Consulting Group
marketwi.com

Measure Consumer
Perspective *measurecp.com*

Michelson & Associates
michelson.com

Mystery Guest
grassrootsmeasures.com

Quality Ass. Mystery Shopper
qams.com

Rentrak
ms.rentrak.com

Restaurant Cops
restaurant-cops.com

Perception Strategies
perstrat.com

Person to Person
persontopersonquality.com

Personal Profiles, Inc.
ppiadvantage.com

Pied Piper Management Co.
carmysteryshopper.com

Pinnacle Financial Strategies
sassieshop.com

Premier Mystery Shopping
secretshopper.com

Premier Service
premierservice.ca

Pulseback
pulseback.com

Shoppers Critique
International
shopperscritique.com

Shoppers Inc.
shopperjobs.com

Signature Worldwide
signatureworldwide.com

Retail Track
retailtrack.com

RQA, Inc.
rqa-inc.com

Second to None
second-to-none.com

Sentry Marketing
sentrymarketing.com

Service Excellence Group
serviceexcellencegroup.com

Service Metrics Group
servicemetricsgroup.com

Service Performance Group
spgweb.com

Service Scouts
servicescouts.com

Service Research Corporation
serviceresearch.com

Shoppers Confidential Inc.

Sinclair Customer Metrics
sinclaircustomermetrics.com

Spies in Disguise
spiesindisguise.com

Stericycle
stericycle.com

Strategic Reflections
strategicreflections.com

The Secret Shopper Company
secretshoppercompany.com

Texas Shoppers Network, Inc.
texasshoppersnetwork.com

Trend Source
trendsource.com

Verify International
verifyinternational.com

Xzamcorp
xzamcorp.com

shoppersconfidential.com

Table 11-2 Scheduling Companies

BLD Scheduling	*bldschedulers.com*
Coast to Coast Scheduling Services	*ctscc.com*
Kern Scheduling Services	*kernscheduling.com*
Palm Scheduling Services	*palmschedulingservices.com*
Summit Scheduling & Editing	*summitschedulingservices.com*

Additional Resources

http://volition.com/mystery - A message board that lists hundreds of reputable mystery shopping companies, advice, forums, tips and feedback

http://mysteryshop.org - Mystery Shopping Professional Association, a good place to learn more about getting started as a mystery shopper.

http:/quirks.com - A free online directory of over 300 mystery shopping companies.

Figure 11-1 Sample Mystery Shop Report

Greeting

Did the sales associate greet you with a smile?

☐ Yes

☐ No

If they were busy did they acknowledge you immediately?

☐ Yes

☐ No

Was the associate wearing a name tag?

☐ Yes

☐ No

What was the name of the associate that waited on you?

Service and Environment

How long did you wait for your order to be taken?

☐ Immediate service

☐ Less than 1 minute

☐ 1 to 3 minutes

☐ More than 3 minutes

How long did you wait for your product after ordering?

☐ Less than 1 minute

☐ 1 to 3 minutes

☐ 3 to 5 minutes

☐ More than 5 minutes

How many customers were in line?

Was the store clean and inviting?

☐ Yes

☐ No

Summary

Briefly describe your overall shopping experience.

12

Video Mystery Shopper

EMPLOYMENT STATUS Independent Contractor

EXPERIENCE REQUIRED Some/Many Opportunities for Free Training

OVERVIEW

Video mystery shopping *(also called covert mystery shoppers)* is mystery shopping combined with the use of covert video equipment. You basically secretly record the mystery shopping assignment using video or audio equipment.

The assignments are called "video shops" and they are performed unannounced using video equipment that is hidden on your body or carried in your purse or bag. The completed video shops are uploaded and submitted online to the mystery shopping company.

Video mystery shopping is another one of the more lucrative ways to earn extra money. It's becoming more popular because video mystery shop reports are more reliable than handwritten reports. It's not uncommon to make $1,500 or more a month working part-time doing video shops.

Businesses that use video mystery shoppers include:

- High end retail stores
- Hotels
- Car Rental Agencies
- Apartment Complexes
- Fitness centers and Spas
- Real Estate Agencies
- Tanning Salons

It takes a little more time and effort to get started as video mystery shopper. Some companies prefer to only hire experienced video shoppers but there are companies that offer free training.

As a part of your training, you are taught how to use the equipment and complete a mystery shop. Most companies will have you to do some test shops before assigning you a real shop to help you get used to using the equipment.

Some companies provide the video equipment and other require you to have your own equipment. Some companies may require a deposit before shipping you their equipment. This is just done as a safety measure, in the event that the equipment is lost, stolen or damaged

WORK SCHEDULE

Accepting assignments as a video mystery shopper works exactly the same as regular mystery shopping. You have the freedom and flexibility to choose which jobs you want to work and when you want to work them, just as long as it's completed by the due date. Most video shop assignments are conducted in businesses that are open 7 days a week.

Typical assignments can include:

- Evaluating an employee's sales presentation skills
- Evaluating employee(s) customer service skills
- Recording images of the sales floor and/or service area
- Recording interaction with employee(s) to evaluate if company policy and procedures are being followed

WHAT YOU CAN EXPECT TO EARN

Video shops are a little more complicated than regular traditional mystery shopping assignments and take longer to do so the pay is much higher. Fees can range from $25-$400 per assignment. As with traditional mystery shopping, the amount you are paid is based on the complexity of the assignment. A normal assignment can take anywhere from 30 minutes to 2 hours to complete.

Hypothetical Video Mystery Shopping Assignments:

- Your assignment is to go to a local department store and secretly record the interaction between you and a specified employee. This assignment could take up to 15 to 30 minutes to complete. It pays $35.00

- Your assignment is to meet with a homebuilder, posing as a potential customer looking to purchase a home in a new subdivision. You are to secretly record the entire meeting. This assignment could last up to 90 minutes. It pays $145.00.

PAY STRUCTURE

See Chapter 11- PAY STRUCTURE.

DRAWBACKS

1. If the recording is not up to the standard or not completed as instructed, then you won't get paid for your time and effort.
2. If you experience technical problems with the equipment during a shop that is not your fault, you won't get paid.
3. Opportunities can be limited if you don't' live in or near a major city or live in a rural area.
4. See Drawbacks Chapter 11.

REQUIREMENTS TO GET STARTED

- ✓ At least 18 years old
- ✓ Have access to the internet
- ✓ Have access to video recording equipment
- ✓ Have access to reliable transportation
- ✓ Have an email address

FINDING OPPORTUNITIES

Not all mystery shopping companies perform video shops. The quickest way to find opportunities is to register with VSN, videoshoppingnetwork.org. VSN is a networking organization that was created for the video mystery shopping community. VSN offers a forum and free training for anyone that wants to become a video mystery shopper

Other ways to find opportunities include:

- Register with several Free Mystery Shopping Job boards
- Register with several Mystery Shopping scheduling services
- Do an inquiry on traditional Mystery Shopping Forums

TIME-SAVING/MONEY MAKING TIPS

Read the guidelines and instructions very carefully before accepting an assignment. Only accept assignments that you are comfortable performing and feel you can complete. Companies pay a lot of money for video shops. Not following instructions or completing a shop as expected will result in you not get paid and/or getting fewer assignments

Purchase your own equipment. After you have done a few video shops and feel comfortable doing them, you may want to consider buying your own equipment. It will be well worth the investment. Having your own equipment increases your chances of getting more assignments and making extra money from bonuses for doing last minute shops with quick deadlines

Complete several traditional mystery shops. If you are new to mystery shopping, completing a few traditional shops will help you better understand the industry

KEYWORD SEARCH

For best search results, enter any of the following keywords:

- Video Mystery Shopper
- Video Secret Shopper
- Video Mystery Shop Jobs
- Video Shopping
- Video Mystery Shopping Companies
- Covert Video Mystery Shopper

Table 12-1 Video Mystery Shopper Opportunities

*Advanced Feedback
advancedfeedback.com

*All-Star Customer Service
mysteryshoppingexperts.com

*Bare International
bareinternational.com

Baird Group
baird-group.com

BDS Marketing Inc.
bdsmktg.com

BestMark.com
bestmark.com

Business Observations
businessobservations.com

*Clear Evaluations
clearevalutions.com

Confero
conferoinc.com

Customer Impact
customerimpactinfo.com

LeBlanc & Associates
mleblanc.com

Measure Consumer Perspectives
measurecp.com

Melinda Brody & Associates
melindabrody.com

Michaels & Associates
ispyforyou.com

Personal Profiles, Inc.
newhomemysteryshops.com

Quality Assessments
qams.com

Retail Track
retailtrack.com

Second To None
second-to-none.com

Shopper's View
shoppersview.com

Sinclair Customer Metrics
sinclaircustomermetrics.com

Ellis Partners
ellismysteryshopperjobs.com

The Shadow Agency
theshadowagency.com

*Game Film Consultants
gamefilmconsultants.com

The Training Factor
thetrainingfactor.com

Impact Marketing
impact-mrkt.com

Trend Source
trendsource.com

InteliChek
intelichek.com

Xzamcorp
xzamcorp.com

*Offers free training

13

Hospitality Evaluator

EMPLOYMENT STATUS Independent Contractor

EXPERIENCE REQUIRED Little to None

OVERVIEW

Hospitality evaluators are mystery shoppers that perform specialized secret shops in the hospitality industry. The hospitality segment is a large piece of the growing mystery shopping industry.

Performing hospitality evaluations is one of the more pleasurable and rewarding ways of earning extra money. In addition to enjoying the benefits of higher payer assignments, you get great perks like free nights at a hotel, free spa treatments, free meals at high restaurants, etc.

Secret shops are performed in such places as:

- Hotels
- Spas
- Cruise ships
- Casinos
- Resorts
- High end restaurants
- Private clubs
- Time Shares

WORK SCHEDULE

The work is basically the same as traditional mystery shopping. You have the freedom to create your own work schedule. You decide which shops are most convenient for you to complete. After you accept the assignment, you perform the shop as instructed and submit your report online by the due date.

Typical assignments can include:

- Evaluating the quality of service
- Ordering a particular meal and evaluating the quality of the food
- Inspecting room accommodations
- Making a complaint about your services and observing how you were treated

WHAT YOU CAN EXPECT TO EARN

Fees can range from $35 up to $500 plus reimbursement depending on the assignment. Some shops may not include a fee but only reimburse for your expenses, but the reimbursement could be $60, $75, $150 or more.

Examples:

An assignment at a local high- end restaurant does not include a fee but will reimburse the cost of a meal up to $200.00.

A hotel assignment at the Marriott requires an overnight stay. The fee is $75.00 plus reimbursement up to $125.00.

An assignment at the Casino pays $80.00 plus reimbursement up to $50.00

DRAWBACKS

1. Competition is stiff for the best assignments
2. Some mystery shopping companies have strict limits on the number of time you can conduct a shop. In many cases, you can only evaluate a particular business once, or once a year, etc.
3. Opportunities for higher paying assignments may be limited, if you live in a rural area
4. Some higher paying assignments may require you to use your debit or credit card to pay for the expenses that are reimbursed
5. Some companies prefer to only hire shoppers that have experience in the hospitality industry

REQUIREMENTS TO GET STARTED

- ✓ At 18 years old
- ✓ Have access to reliable transportation
- ✓ Have access to a computer with internet connection
- ✓ An email address
- ✓ Have access to a scanner or fax to submit copies of paper reports
- ✓ Have access to a digital camera or cell phone with a camera

FINDING OPPORTUNITIES

See also Chapter 11- Finding Opportunities

A WORD OF CAUTION

Remember, you can protect yourself from scammers by not doing business with companies that:

- ✖ Require you to pay a fee for certification in order to accept assignments
- ✖ Charge a fee to access "hidden" mystery shopping opportunities
- ✖ Sell directories of companies that hire mystery shopping companies
- ✖ Solicit you without permission via email
- ✖ Ask you to deposit a check and then wire some of the money back to them

Real mystery shopping companies don't charge fees to get started or to access their job boards.

KEYWORD SEARCH

For best search results, enter any of the following keywords:

- Hospitality Evaluators
- Hotel Mystery Shopper Jobs
- Hospitality Secret Shopper
- Hospitality Mystery Shopping Company
- High End Mystery Shops
- Hotel Mystery Shops

You can also search for opportunities in specific industries such as:

- Spa Mystery Shopping
- Casino Mystery Shopping
- Restaurant Mystery Shopping

Table 13-1 Hospitality Evaluator Opportunities

A Closer Look
a-closer-look.com

Eye Spy Critique & Consulting
eyespycc.com

Advance Feedback
advancefeedback.com

Five Diamond Hospitality
fivediamondhospitality.com

Bare International
bareinternational.com

Gapbuster
gapbuster.com

BestMark
bestmark.com

Goodwin Hospitality Shopper
mysteryshopperprogram.com

Bevinco
bevinco.com

Guest Check
theguestcheck.com

Beyond Hello
beyondhello.com

Hotel Shopping Network
hotelshoppingnetwork.com

Buckalew Hospitality
buckalewhospitality.com

HS Brands International
hsbrands.com

Cirrus
cirrusmktg.com

I-Spy Hospitality Audit Svc
ispy4u.net

Count On Us
ucountonus.com

Imyst
imyst.com

Coyle Hospitality
coylehospitality.com

Inside Evaluators
insideevaluators.com

Customer Impact
customerimpactinfo.com

Its Incognito
itsincognito.com

Data Quest Ltd
dataquestonline.com

Dynamic Advantage
dynamic-advantage.com

ESP Shop
espshop.com

Expert Audits
stericycleexpertsolutions.com

MSP Services LLC
mysteryshopperpros.com

Mystery Guest
grassrootsmeasures.com

National Shopping Service
nationalshoppingservice.com

NSite
nsite.com

Person to Person Quality
persontopersonquality.com

Phantom Shoppers
phantom-shoppers.com

QSI Specialists
qsispecialists.com

Quality Assessments
qams.com

LRA Worldwide
lraworldwide.com

Management Consultant Group
managementconsultantgroup.com

Maritz Research
maritzresearch.com

MSI Mystery Shopping
mysteryshopmsi.com

Sentry Marketing
sentrymarketing.com

Service Check
servicecheck.com

Service Excellence Group
serviceexcellencegroup.com

Service Impressions
serviceimpressions.com

Service Performance Group
spgweb.com

Service Scouts
servicescouts.com

Shoppers Confidential Inc.
shoppersconfidential.com

Shoppers Critique
shopperscritique.com

Quality Assurance Consulting
qacinc.com

Quest for Best
questforbest.com

Reality Check
rcmysteryshopper.com

Reflection
reflectionsms.com

Regal Hospitality Group
regalhospitalitygroup.com

Restaurant Cops
restaurant-cops.com

Satisfaction Services Inc.
satisfactionservices.com

Secret Shopper
secretshopper.com

Signature Worldwide
signatureworldwide.com

Spies in Disguise
spiesindisguise.com

SQM
sqm.ca

The Brandt Group
thebrandtgroup.com

The Brandt Group
thebrandtgroup.com

The Performance Edge
pedge.com

Verify International
verifyinternational.com

Xzamcorp
xzamcorp.com

Figure 13-1 Sample Hotel Evaluation Form

Visit Information	Response
1. Check-in date	04/22/14
2. Check-out date	04/23/14
5. Time of check-in	3:15 p.m.
6. Time of check-out	11:30 a.m.
7. Total amount for room	137.00

Reservations	Response
1. Name of receptionist	Janice
2. Was the telephone answered in a prompt and professional manner?	YES
3. Was the receptionist genuinely accommodating to your arrival time, date, and room size?	YES
4. Were you given a confirmation number along with a repeat of the arrival/departure date and rate?	YES

Reservation Summary

After two rings, Janice answered the phone. I said I needed a room for April 22. She asked me to wait while she checked to see if a room was available for that date. She asked if I wanted smoking or non-smoking and if I said non-smoking king. She then said she had rooms available for $89 and $109. She said the $109 rooms had a view. I booked the $109 room. She asked if I was a preferred guest member and I said I was not. She said they usually automatically enroll all customers and asked if I was interested. I said yes and she enrolled me at that time.

She asked how I would like to guarantee the room and I told her with my visa card and gave her my credit card information. Janice repeated all of the reservation information, advised me about the sales tax and then provided my confirmation number.

She asked if there was anything else she could do for me, thanked me and told me to enjoy my trip. Her demeanor was professional and friendly.

WORK AT HOME OPPORTUNITIES

Positive Thoughts
Generate
Positive Feelings
And
Attract Positive Life
Experiences

14

Telephone Mystery Shopper

EMPLOYMENT STATUS Independent Contractor

EXPERIENCE REQUIRED None

OVERVIEW

Telephone mystery shopping is essentially the same as mystery shopping with the exception that all of the assignments are performed over the phone. It's actually easier than regular mystery shopping because all of the work is done from the convenience of your home. This is an extremely convenient to earn extra money especially, if you live in a rural area, don't drive, are home-bound or don't have access to transportation.

Performing telephone mystery shops can also be very intriguing. The work involves placing calls to businesses posing as a customer and evaluating your experience based on your instructions. Assignments are generally very simple and don't require a lot of time to complete.

Most companies only require you to take notes during the call. Others may require you to record the shop. In that case, the mystery shopping company will have you to call a special toll number to make the call or download software onto your computer.

Many types of companies use mystery phone shoppers to help improve their customer service, including:

- Car Dealerships
- Travel Agencies
- Apartment Complexes
- High End Retail Shops

Some companies even use telephone mystery shopping as a way to spy on their competition.

WORK SCHEDULE

Just like regular mystery shopping, you have the option of choosing which assignments you want to complete. Some assignments may require you to call a business during certain hours or only on certain days. Other than that, once you accept an assignment, you have the flexibility to complete the assignment at your convenience just as long as it's done and reported by the due date.

Typical assignments can include:

- Reporting if the telephone was answered in three rings or less
- Evaluating how you were greeted
- Obtaining information about a certain product or service
- Measuring the amount of time you were left on hold

WHAT YOU CAN EXPECT TO EARN

The fee you are paid as a mystery phone shopper is not as high as working as a traditional mystery shopper. Fees can range from $3-$15 per call. A normal assignment can take anywhere from 15 seconds to 20 minutes to complete.

PAY STRUCTURE

See Chapter 11-PAY STRUCTURE.

DRAWBACKS

1. You will need to sign up with several different companies to earn more than $200.00 a month
2. Because telephone mystery shopping jobs are so easy, the higher paying assignments can go very quickly

HYPOTHETICAL TELEPHONE MYSTERY SHOPPING ASSIGNMENTS:

- Your assignment is to call AAA travel agency and inquire about a vacation special for you and your family. This phone call will not be recorded so you will need to take notes. This assignment could take up to 20 minutes to complete. It pays $15.00

- Your assignment is to call Sears and make any inquiry to evaluate how many times the phone rang and the employee's phone greeting. This will be a recorded phone call. The assignment could last up to 5 minutes. It pays $5.00.

- Your assignment is to call an apartment complex posing as a potential customer looking for a two bedroom apartment and to evaluate the leasing agent's sales skills. This is not a recorded shop. The assignment could last up to 20 minutes. It pays $12.00.

REQUIREMENTS TO GET STARTED

- ✓ Have access to the interne
- ✓ Have an email address
- ✓ Have access to a telephone

FINDING OPPORTUNITIES

Not all Mystery shopping companies perform telephone mystery shops. The quickest way to find companies that offer telephone assignments is to:

1. Do a search on **Quirks.com** for Mystery Shopping companies that offer audio recorded shops
2. Register with several free Mystery shopping job boards like **JobSlinger.com** or **MSJobBoard.com**
3. Register with several Mystery Shopping scheduling services
4. Do an inquiry on Mystery Shopping Forums

KEYWORD SEARCH

For best search results, enter any of the following keywords:

- Telephone Mystery Shoppers
- Mystery Caller Jobs
- Telephone Secret Shopper
- Mystery Shopper Telephone Evaluator
- Secret Caller Jobs
- Phone Shopper Jobs

Table 14-1 Telephone Mystery Shopper Opportunities

Ace Mystery Shopping
acemysteryshopping.com

Customer Perspectives
customerperspectives.com

Advanced Feedback
advancedfeedback.com

Devon Hill
devonhillassociates.com

Amusement Guest Experience
amusementadvantage.com

DSG Associates
dsgai.com

Ann Michaels & Associates
ishopforyou.com

Dynamic Advantage
dynamic-advantage.com

Anonymous Insights Inc.
a-sights.com

Ellis Partners
epmsonline.com

Apartment Shoppe
apartmentmysteryshopper.com

Game Film Consultants
gamefilmconsultants.com

Arc
arllc.com

Imyst
imyst.com

Assurance Performance
apartmentmysteryshoppers.com

Inteli Chek
intelichek.com

Bare International
bareinternational.com

Intelli-Shop
intelli-shop.com

BestMark.com
bestmark.com

I Secret Shop
isecretshop.com

Bild & Company
tracibild.com

Measure Consumer Perspectives
measurecp.com

BMA Mystery Shopping
mystery-shopping.com

Remington Evaluations
remysteryshops.com

The Brandt Group
thebrandtgroup.com

Ritter & Associates
ritterassociates.com

Confero
conferoinc.com

Secret Shopper
secretshopper.com

Coranet Evaluations Inc.
coranetevaluations.com

Service Performance Group
spgweb.com

Shadow Agency
theshadowagency.com

Technology Store Shopper
technologystoreshopper.com

Shopper's Critique
shopperscritique.com

Telexpertise
telexpertise.com

Shopper's View
shoppersview.com

Test Track Research
testtrackresearch.com

Sinclair Customer Metrics
sinclaircustomermetrics.com

Trend Source
trendsource.com

Sparks Research
sparksresearch.com

Xzamcorp
xzamcorp.com

Sutter Marketing Inc.
suttermarketing.com

15

At- Home Freelance Agent

EMPLOYMENT STATUS Independent Contractor

EXPERIENCE REQUIRED Some/Many Opportunities for New Freelancers

OVERVIEW

At home freelance agents (*also call subcontractors*) are independent contractors that perform one time projects for specific clients.
Work projects vary widely and can include almost anything such as:

- Customer Service Projects
- Making calls
- Event Planning
- Designing Websites
- Performing Research
- Doing voice overs
- Creating Documents
- Creating Videos'
- Editing and proofreading
- Creating sales materials
- Creating SEO reports
- Translating
- Online Marketing
- Trend-spotting

This can be a really great way to earn extra money. Thanks to the internet, there are endless opportunities to make money doing freelance work. It's one of the fastest growing "work at home" income opportunities. Depending on how much time you commit and your skill set, you have the potential to make $1,000 or more a month working part-time.

WORK SCHEDULE

You are in complete control. You decide what projects you want to complete and what days you want to work. Since, freelance agents generally complete a project and move on to the next project. Clients aren't concerned how and when you do the work, just as long as your work is completed by the project deadline.

WHAT YOU CAN EXPECT TO EARN

Freelance agents are paid in a wide variety of rate structures:

- Per project basis
- Per hour
- Per call
- Per word for freelance writers
- Flat fee or lump sum

Rates are often negotiated and based on the type of project, the project's time line and your skill set. Fees can start as low as $5 for a simple project and go as high as $500 or more for complex projects.

Hypothetical Freelance Project Postings:

- Need someone to research requested PDF documents for a writing project. Will send you the requested documents by email. Project deadline: 2 weeks. Pay rate: $15 per document

- Need someone set-up database of email contacts. Project deadline: 3 weeks. Pay rate: $250 flat

- Need someone to record a voice over from a written script. Deadline: 3 days. Pay rate: $10

PAY STRUCTURE

Pay methods vary in accordance to how you obtain your work. If you obtain your work from a freelance website company, then you will be paid via direct deposit or PayPal. Most freelance websites pay once a week or bi-monthly.

If you obtain work directly from a client or company, then you will be paid in accordance with the terms of agreement of the work contract.

DRAWBACKS

1. It can take a couple of weeks to get your first good paying jobs
2. There's a lot of competition for the higher paying jobs
3. The workload can be unpredictable – you might have three deadlines one week and one the next week

REQUIREMENTS TO GET STARTED

- ✓ Have access to a computer with internet
- ✓ Scanner or fax
- ✓ An email address
- ✓ A small website to market your services (optional)

FINDING OPPORTUNITIES

The quickest way to find opportunities is by signing up with several online freelance websites. You can start by creating a **free** account to gain access to the available jobs.

HERE'S HOW THE PROCESS WORKS:

Step 1 You register online at the freelance company's website to create your free account

Step 2 After setting up your account, you can search for open projects

Step 3 To obtain work, you bid on the projects that you can complete and then wait for the client to accept or negotiate your bid

Step 4 If you win the bid, then you start the work.

Step 5 Once the projected is completed to the client's satisfaction, you get paid!

 *A WORD OF CAUTION*

As with anything that becomes extremely popular online, along comes the scams. And you will find plenty on the road of freelance opportunities. To protect yourself from scammers, beware of sites or ads that contain any of the following:

* ✘ Exaggerated income claims
* ✘ Claims you can make a lot of money for little or no work
* ✘ Secret inside information
* ✘ Requires you to pay before you get the information

You can always check out any company with the Better Business Bureau and/or by doing a Google search to view any past issues or complaints posted online.

KEYWORD SEARCH

For best search results, enter any of the following keywords:

* Work at Home Contract Jobs
* Online Freelance Websites
* At Home Freelance Jobs
* Work at Home Independent Agent
* Work at Home Freelance Jobs
* Work at Home Part-time jobs

Table 15-1 At Home Freelance Agent Opportunities

Billing Services Group (BSG)	bsgclearing.com
Clicknwork	clicknwork.com
ContractWorld.jobs	contractworld.jobs
CSR Virtual Staffing	csrvirtualstaffing.com
Elance	elance.com
Freelancer	freelancer.com
Guru	guru.com
Leapforce At Home	leapforceathome.com
Lionbridge	lionbridge.com
ODesk	odesk.com
People Per Hour	peopleperhour.com
Verafast	verafast.com
Workhoppers	workhoppers.com

16

Online Writer

EMPLOYMENT STATUS Independent Contractor

EXPERIENCE REQUIRED Some/Plenty Opportunities for New Writers

OVERVIEW

Writing for the web is by far is one of the easiest ways to make extra money. It's another one of the fastest growing "work at home" opportunities. And once again, thanks to the internet, there are endless opportunities to earn extra money writing online.

Projects can include:

- Writing articles
- Blogging
- Ghost Writing Books
- Creating Content
- Creating EBooks
- Writing Reviews
- Writing Buying Guides
- Writing Product Descriptions

You don't need a degree to get started as a writer. Some companies require prior writing experience. But there are many sites that simply require that you have good grammar and meet their writing skill requirements. Most sites and clients will require you to submit a writing sample or take a writing test.

WORK SCHEDULE

What's great about writing is that you are in complete control. You decide what projects you want to complete, the days and hours you want to work. It doesn't matter when you work, just as long as your project is completed by its deadline. If you write more you earn more.

WHAT YOU CAN EXPECT TO EARN

Fees vary widely. They are based on the type of project, your skill set and the project's time line. Fees can range from .01-.11 cent per word for a 500 word article and can go as high as $1,500 or more for a ghost writing or more complex project.

PAY STRUCTURE

If you obtain your work from a freelance website company, then you will be paid via direct deposit or PayPal. Most sites pay once a week or bi-weekly.

If you obtain your work directly from a client or company, then you will be paid in accordance with the terms of agreement of the work contract.

DRAWBACKS

1. If you don't have experience, it can take a couple of weeks to get your first good paying job
2. There's a lot of competition for the higher paying jobs
3. You may have to take several lower paying jobs to gain experience or build your portfolio.

REQUIREMENTS TO GET STARTED

- ✓ Have access to a computer with internet
- ✓ An email address
- ✓ Good grammar skills
- ✓ Good typing skills
- ✓ A portfolio of writing samples
- ✓ A small website to market your services (optional)

FINDING OPPORTUNITIES

There many of ways to find writing opportunities. You can sign up for a free account on many of the freelance writing sites.

You can also find opportunities on:

- Craigslist
- Job Boards like Indeed, Monster or Simply Hired
- Facebook Freelance Writing Groups
- Linkedin
- Redditt
- Forums for Writers like: Writer's Digest.com

 A WORD OF CAUTION

- ✖ There are sites that will charge you a fee to find real writing jobs. Some are worth the fee and others are just scams. You can find plenty of real writing jobs for free. It may take a while to weed through the lower paying assignments but it won't cost you anything if you are on a budget.

✖ To protect yourself, stick with websites that are widely known. You can always do a google search and check online reviews if you have concerns about a particular company or website.

TIME-SAVING/MONEY MAKING TIPS

If you don't have any experience, writing articles, reviews and guest blogging are the easiest way to start making money writing.

To increase your chances of getting assignments, sign up for many different types of freelance writing sites.

Hone your skills by studying and mimicking (not copying) the writing style of popular bloggers and writers.

KEYWORD SEARCH

For best search results, enter any of the following keywords:

- Freelance Writers Wanted
- Article Writers Needed
- Content Writer Jobs
- Article Writers Wanted
- Writer Jobs Online
- Get Paid to Write
- Work from Home Writing Jobs for Beginners
- Work from Home Writing Jobs no fees
- Freelance Writing Gigs
- Guest Bloggers Wanted

Table 16-1 Online Writer Opportunities

About.com	about.com
*Amazon Turk	mturk.com
BreakStudios.com	breakstudios.break.com
College Humor	collegehumor.com
Cracked.com	cracked.com
*CrowdSource	crowdsource.com
*Demand Media Studio	create.demandstudios.com
Editfast	editfast.com
Freelancewriting	freelancewriting.com
Elance	elance.com
Fiverr	fiverr.com
Freelancer	freelancer.com
*Iwriter.com	iwriter.com
*Listverse	listvers.com
MediaBistro.com	mediabistro.com
Odesk	Odesk.com
People Per Hour	Peopleperhour.com
Scripted	scripted.com
Strong Whispers	strongwhispers.com
Writertown	writertown.com
Textbroker	textbroker.com
The Content Authority	thecontentauthority.com
Tutsplus	tutsplus.com
*Zerys	zerys.com

*Good for beginners-pays lower fees

Figure 16-1 Sample Article

What is Cellulite?

If you are like most women, you have probably lived through this moment. You finally break out your stunning, new miniskirt. And you are rocking it, until you sit down, cross your legs and look down to notice that the skin on your thighs resembles the surface of the moon.

Those dimples have put a hitch in the swagger of many a Diva's and church-ladies, alike. What's more, those unsavory little divots have spurred a billion dollar industry for creams and wraps to injectable snake oils that promise their permanent eradication. Many a money savvy woman has fallen for false claims because, in reality, most of us don't exactly understand what it is we are dealing with.

Cellulite, Demystified...

So what is cellulite, really? Cellulite is caused by the breakdown of the collagen structure that holds your fat stores in place. To understand it, imagine that your fat stores are like a hard- boiled egg and your collagen is like panty hose. When you are younger, your collagen fibers are tightly knit together, like your, standard, nude variety of panty hose. If you were to wrap an egg in this type of material, the surface of the egg would remain smooth, even when the hose are pulled tightly over it. As we age, our collagen fibers start to break down and become more loosely knit together, resembling something more like fishnet stockings. Of course, you can imagine, when you press the fishnet stockings over the surface of the egg, you get a much different pattern of indentions and bulges.

This is what is happening with your cellulite. As you age, your collagen fibers are less able to hold back the fat behind them, allowing portions of fat to bulge out. This effect is intensified when stress is applied to the collagen mesh, as it is when you sit down and cross your legs.

What Causes Cellulite?

For most of us cellulite, or at least the breakdown of collagen, is inevitable. There are a few factors that make it worse.

More Fat = More Cellulite- As you might imagine, when there is more fat behind the collagen mesh, the mesh has a harder time holding it back, making the dimples more visible.

Poor Circulation- Your collagen begins to break down because it is not being adequately supplied with nutrients from your blood. This can happen because the blood vessels are being constricted unnaturally by causes like:

Smoking- As if you needed another reason to quit.

Remaining seated for long periods of time- There is a reason why you first spot cellulite in the areas that you sit on.

Constrictive undergarments- Save the Spanx for date night!

Lack of muscle mass- Muscles have 85% more blood vessels than fat tissue.

Poor Nutrition- Even if you have tons of blood flow to the affected area, if you aren't providing your body with the essential tools, like protein and antioxidants, needed to rebuild the deteriorating collagen, you won't be able to reverse the dimpling.

But what's the most important fact that you need to know, about cellulite? Cellulite happens to almost 90% of all women. It's the great equalizer, so don't let it steal your swagger!

Courtesy of the web

17

Virtual Assistant

EMPLOYMENT STATUS Independent Contractor

EXPERIENCE REQUIRED Office Administration Skills

OVERVIEW

Virtual assistants are office assistants that work from home. They provide administrative, creative or technical services generally to small businesses that need help running their business. This is another great way to earn extra money if you are homebound or live in a rural area and have the skills needed to do the work.

Tasks vary and can include:

- Handling inquiries by phone or email
- Maintaining a calendar and setting up meetings
- Making travel arrangements
- Making PowerPoint Presentations
- Preparing and sending out email newsletters
- Sending out requested information to customers via mail
- Conducting research
- Creating documents
- Proofreading
- Posting online
- Overseeing online projects
- Conducting Research

WORK SCHEDULE

You have the freedom to choose when and how much you want to work. Your work hours are based on the needs of your clients. Some assignments may require you to work during certain hours of the day or on specific days of the week.

Some clients may have a web based workspace, giving you the ability to access documents, share files and collaborate on projects, anytime, anywhere.

WHAT YOU CAN EXPECT TO EARN

The rate that you are paid is generally based on the complexity of the work. The pay can range between $15 and $45 per hour.

PAY STRUCTURE

Payment methods vary. Most companies offer direct deposit and pay twice a month.

DRAWBACKS

1. It may take a couple of weeks to get your first few jobs.
2. Some companies/clients may prefer to only hire someone with a college degree or several years of experience.

REQUIREMENTS TO GET STARTED

- ✓ Computer with up to date software
- ✓ Internet connection
- ✓ Phone with voicemail or answering machine
- ✓ Access to fax or scanner

✓ Proficient with Microsoft software, using email attachments, uploading and downloading files

FINDING OPPORTUNITIES

Most companies post job opening on their websites. Some small business owners run ads on Craigslist. The ads are generally listed in the job section under administration or part-time jobs.

You can also find opportunities:

- On job boards like Indeed, Monster or Simply Hired
- On forums like VA Networking
- By joining Virtual Assistant Facebook groups
- By doing a job search on Linked

A WORD OF CAUTION

There are sites that will try to charge you a membership fee to find virtual assistant job opening. You can find plenty of jobs for free. To protect yourself, stick with websites that are widely known. You can always do a google search and check online reviews if you have concerns about a particular company, website or service.

KEYWORD SEARCH

For best search results, enter any of the following keywords:

- Virtual Assistants
- Virtual Assistant Companies
- Virtual Staffing
- Virtual Assistant Websites
- Virtual Assistant Needed

Table17-1 Virtual Assistant Opportunities

Contemporary Virtual Assistants	contemporaryva.com
CSR Virtual Staffing	csrvitualstaffing.com
Elance	elance.com
Fancy Hands	fancyhands.com
Freelance	freelance.com
ODesk	odesk.com
Task Army	taskarmy.com
Virtual Assistant for Experts	vaforexperts.com
Virtual Gal Friday	virtualgalfriday.com
Virtual Pros Staffing	virtualpros.com
Virtual Staffing Team	virtualstaffingteam.com
Worldwide 101	worldwide101.com
Zirtual	zirtual.com

18

Online Tutor

EMPLOYMENT STATUS Independent Contractor

EXPERIENCE REQUIRED Prior Teaching, Tutoring or Completed 2-3 Years College

OVERVIEW

Online tutoring is a great way to earn extra money if you are a college student, professional, teacher or are an expert in a certain field. The work is extremely rewarding and can be another excellent way to earn money if you are homebound or live in a rural area.

The requirements vary. Most companies require a college degree but it doesn't have to be in a specific field. Some companies may require you to have prior teaching, tutoring experience or have completed 2-3 years of college

WORK SCHEDULE

In most cases, you have the freedom to choose the hours you want to work. All of the tutoring sessions are online. Various online tools are used to allow the student and tutor to easily communicate with one another. This can include video chatting, whiteboard, web conferencing, teleconferencing and other outlets.

WHAT YOU CAN EXPECT TO EARN

Pay rates vary. The average rate of pay is between $15 and $18 an hour. Some sites let you set your own rates.

PAY STRUCTURE

Most companies offer direct deposit or pay via PayPal and pay twice a month.

REQUIREMENTS TO GET STARTED

- ✓ Computer with up to date software
- ✓ Internet connection
- ✓ A Valid email address
- ✓ Proficient with Microsoft software, using email attachments, uploading and downloading files
- ✓ Strong oral and written communication skills
- ✓ Proficient with Microsoft software, using email attachments, uploading and downloading files

FINDING OPPORTUNITIES

Most companies post openings on their websites. Quite a few run ads online or on job boards like Indeed, Monster, Simply Hired.

KEYWORD SEARCH

For best search results, enter any of the following keywords:

- Online Tutoring Jobs
- Home Based Tutor Jobs Online
- Online Tutoring Companies Hiring
- Online Tutor Positions
- How to Become an Online Tutor
- Online Tutoring Jobs for college students

Table 18-1 Online Tutor Opportunities

Aim Academics	aim4a.com/tutors.php
Buddy School	buddyschool.com
Chegg Study	chegg.com/homework
EAge	eagetutor.com
Ed2net	ed2netlearning.com
EduNiche	eduniche.com
ETutor.com	e-tutor.com
Growing Stars	growingstars.com
InstantEdu	instaedu.com
Isus	jobs.ispeakuspeak.com
Jer Group	eronline.com
Kaplan Kids	kaplankids.com
Live Person	liveperson.com
Minds Ahead	mindsahead.com
Physics24/7	physics247.com
Promise Cyber School	promise4all.com
Sophia	sophia.org
Study Pool	studypool.com
Transwebtutors	transwebtutors.com
Tutor.com	tutor.com
TutaPoint	tutapoint.com
TutorBee.com	tutorbee.com
Tutor Doctor	tutordoctor.com
Tutor Services	tutorservices.com
TutorVista.com	tutorvista.com
WizIQ	wiziq.com

19

Micro-Job Worker

EMPLOYMENT STATUS Independent Contractor

EXPERIENCE REQUIRED None

OVERVIEW

Micro-job work (also called pay per task jobs) can be anything. It's basically doing a small one-time task for a set amount of money. This is one of the easiest ways to make extra money working online from home.

Most of the tasks sites are easy to use. The tasks are generally simple for the most part. The variety of work is wide and can involve such things as:

- Tagging photos
- Loading YouTube videos
- Writing or editing texts
- Checking the price of milk at local grocery
- Creating email accounts
- Web research
- Verifying information (websites, addresses, etc.)

Some sites may have you to take qualification tests so that they can match you with the tasks that suit your skills.

WORK SCHEDULE

The work schedule is extremely flexible. You have the freedom to choose when and how much you want to work.

WHAT YOU CAN EXPECT TO EARN

The pay rates for micro jobs also vary widely. The amount you earn is based on the job site, the complexity of the job and your skill set. Some jobs pay well and there's those that pay very little. The pay can be as low as $0.01 and as high as $100 per task.

PAY STRUCTURE

Most pay via PayPal or offer direct deposit. A surprisingly number of sites pay weekly or even daily.

DRAWBACKS

1. Some tasks site don't pay that well
2. The work flow can be inconsistent. The work is not always a sure thing
3. Some of the tasks can be a complete waste of your time

REQUIREMENTS TO GET STARTED

✓ Have access to a computer with internet
✓ A cell phone that can take photos
✓ An email address
✓ Access to transportation (some assignments)

FINDING OPPORTUNITIES

Most companies post available assignments on their job boards. You can gain access to their job boards by registering for a free account.

KEYWORD SEARCH

For best search results, enter any of the following keywords

- Micro Worker Sites
- Micro Job Sites
- Pay Per Task Jobs
- Pay Per Task Online Jobs
- Micro-jobsites Marketplace

TIME SAVING/MONEY MAKING TIPS

Be sure to read the FAQ sections before starting a task. You don't want to waste your time and efforts on something that is not worth your time

 Sign up for several websites. Many people do lots of short, easy micro-jobs to create of steady income flow.

Table 19-1 Micro Work Opportunities

Amazon Turk	amazonturk.com
Click Chores	clickchores.com
Click Worker	clickworker.com
Cloud Crowd	cloudcrowd.com
Do My Stuff	domystuff.com
Easy Shift	easyshiftapp.com
Field Agent	fieldagent.net
FittyTown	fittytown.com
Fiver	fiver.com
Fourerr	fourerr.com
GigsBull	gigsbull.com
Gigwalk	gigwalk.com/gigwalkers
Humantic	humantic.net
Loop88	loop88.com
Micro Task	microtask.com
Micro Workers	microworkers.com
Paid2Twitter	paid2twitter.com

Rapid Workers	rapidworkers.com
Slicethepie	slicethepie.com
Task Army	taskarmy.com
Task Rabbit	taskrabbit.com
Twentyville	twentyville.com
Zapiddy	zapiddy.com

20

Website Tester

EMPLOYMENT STATUS Independent Contractor

EXPERIENCE REQUIRED None

OVERVIEW

Website testers (*also known as remote usability testers*) are paid to review selected business websites or mobile applications and give their opinion on the usability of the website or application. This is an easy way to earn extra money but don't expect to make a lot of money.

Website testers are chosen based on their demographic profiles. That means you only get the opportunity to test websites whenever a client requests your particular profile. It's a toss- up because you never know when your profile will be chosen. Some sites may require you to take a small sample test

WORK SCHEDULE

Extremely flexible, you work when it's convenient for you. .

WHAT YOU CAN EXPECT TO EARN

The pay rates range from $5-$10 per test for websites and $15 for mobile applications. Reviews generally take about 15-20 minutes to complete.

PAY STRUCTURE

Most sites pay weekly via PayPal or direct deposit.

DRAWBACKS

1. Opportunities to earn money can be limited. Some sites have more testers than opportunities.
2. You won't get paid if the client is not satisfied with your work.
3. You never know when your profile will be selected.

REQUIREMENTS TO GET STARTED

- ✓ Have access to a computer with internet
- ✓ An email address
- ✓ A webcam (maybe required for some sites)

FINDING OPPORTUNITIES

Most companies post opening on their websites. Some companies run ads online or post opening on Craigslist. Listing can be found in the jobs section under part-time jobs or ETC.

 A WORD OF CAUTION

Watch out for scammers on this one, you don't have to pay a fee to become a website tester.

KEYWORD SEARCH

For best search results, enter any of the following keywords:

- Website Usability Jobs
- Website Testers
- Website Usability Testing Jobs
- Get Paid to Test Websites

Table 20-1 Website Tester Opportunities

Analysia	analysia.com
Roar Web Design	roarwebdesign.com
Start Up Lift	startuplift.com
TryMYUI	trymyui.com
UserFeel	userfeel.com
Userlytics	userlytics.com
User Testing	usertesting.com
uTEST	utest.com
What Users Do	whatusersdo.com
You Eye	join.youeye.com

NOTES

21

Ads Search Quality Rater

EMPLOYMENT STATUS Independent Contractor

EXPERIENCE REQUIRED None

OVERVIEW

Ads Quality raters track the visual quality and content accuracy of online ads. This one sometimes referred to as "search engine evaluators", "internet assessors" or "google raters," is definitely not for everyone.

This is a great way to earn extra money but the work may be too complicated or boring for some people. It involves working on projects that may include examining and analyzing:

- Advertising related data
- Online text
- Web pages
- Photos and images
- Videos
- And any other types of online information

You will be required to take a lengthy test, but you will be given the materials to study before you take the test.

WORK SCHEDULE

You have the freedom to schedule your own work hours along as you work the required minimum number of hours. Some companies allow you to work as much as you want and other companies restrict you to 20 30 hours per week. You can find this information in their FAQ section.

WHAT YOU CAN EXPECT TO EARN

The pay range is between $13 and $15 per hour.

PAY STRUCTURE

Pay dates and methods vary. Some companies pay twice a month and offer direct deposit. Others pay once a month via check. You can also find this information in their FAQ section before applying.

DRAWBACKS

1. Some companies pay monthly by check
2. Work can be boring
3. Some of the work may include you viewing disturbing images such as porn, death photo, decapitation videos, etc.
4. Work opportunities are restricted to one person per household
5. The work flow may not always be consistent.
6. The work is contract based. If your contract is not renewed for whatever reason, that's it.
7. If you are contracted to work with one company, you are restricted from working with any other company that provides this service.

REQUIREMENTS TO GET STARTED

- ✓ Have access to a computer with internet
- ✓ Scanner or fax
- ✓ An email address

FINDING OPPORTUNITIES

Most companies post opening on their websites. A few may run ads online.

KEYWORD SEARCH

For best search results, enter any of the following keywords:

- Search Engine Evaluator
- Social Search Engine Evaluator
- Ads Quality Rater
- Online Internet Assessor
- Search Quality Judge
- Google Rater

Table 21-1 Ads Rater Opportunities

Appen Butler HIll	appen.com
Leapforce	leapforceathome.com
Lionbridge	lionbridge.com
Zero Chaos	zerochaos.com

22

Data Entry

EMPLOYMENT STATUS Independent Contractor

EXPERIENCE REQUIRED None

OVERVIEW

Data entry involves inputting data (alphabetic, numeric, or symbolic) into a company's computer or file system. The work may also require you to verify and/or edit data as it is entered.

Data entry is a general term that is often referred to a number of different jobs that fall under the umbrella of data entry.

This includes:

- Word Processing
- Captioning
- Typing
- Transcribing
- Information Processing
- Medical Coding

Performing data entry work is great for people that are homebound. It's a good way to earn extra money to pay small bills, buy gas or just have some extra spending money in your pockets.

WORK SCHEDULE

You have the freedom to choose which projects you want to work and when you want to work them. You can work at your own pace with most of the freelance projects. Some companies may require you to complete a minimum number projects or work a certain number of hours per week.

WHAT YOU CAN EXPECT TO EARN

The pay structure varies from company to company, such as:

- Hourly wage
- Per-piece
- Keystrokes per hour or keystrokes per minute

The rate you are paid is based on the complexity and skill level needed to complete the project.

PAY RATE EXAMPLES:

General data entry projects pays per-piece, small forms pay an average of 4 to 8 cents per form and large documents pay an average of $5 to $9 per piece.

Transcription projects pay based on the number of lines typed rather than by the number of hours worked. The average per-line ranges from $0.07 to $0.13, which is equivalent to $10 – $30 per hour, depending on your efficiency.

Cautioners are generally paid for each hour of captioning created. The average pay is between $40 and $100 per hour of captioning.

PAY STRUCTURE

Pay methods vary. There are quite a few companies that pay weekly. Most pay via PayPal or mail a check. Others pay once or twice a month.

DRAWBACKS

1. There can be a long waiting list for legitimate companies.
2. Most entry level data entry jobs often pay really low wages.
3. You might be required to purchase equipment for some of the higher payer jobs.

REQUIREMENTS TO GET STARTED

✓ Type at least 60 wpm with accuracy
✓ Have access to a computer with internet
✓ Have an email address
✓ Have knowledge of using e-mail attachments, downloading and uploading files

FINDING OPPORTUNITIES

Most companies post opening on their websites. The quickest way to find genuine opportunities is to register with some of the following freelance, micro job sites or job boards like:

Amazon Turk

Crowdsource

Elance.com

Odesk.com

Guru.com

Freelancer.com

Learn4good

A WORD OF CAUTION

Unfortunately, work at home data entry is another opportunity that is plagued by scammers. You can protect yourself when looking for data entry jobs by following these tips.

Watch out for companies that:

- ✖ Require you to pay a fee for classes, training kits or certifications in order to accept assignments
- ✖ Promises huge salaries i.e. $50.00 an hour
- ✖ Sell directories of companies that hire data entry workers
- ✖ Solicit you without permission via email
- ✖ Require you to pay a monthly fee to get access to higher paying jobs

Real data entry companies don't charge fees for training, certifications or kits to get started. Legitimate companies give you the **work** *first* **and then** *pay you* for doing the work, not the other way around.

KEYWORD SEARCH

For best search results, enter any of the following keywords:

- Legitimate Data Entry Jobs
- Online Data Entry Jobs No Investment
- Work from Home Data Entry Jobs
- Online Data Entry Jobs Work

Table 22-1 Data Entry Opportunities

3Play Media	3playmedia.com
Accutran Global	accutranglobal.com
Axion Data	axiondata.com
Capitol Typing	capitoltyping.com
Click Worker	clickworker.com
CSR Virtual Staffing	csrvirtualstaffing.com
Dion Data Solutions	diondatasolutions.net
Elance	elance.com
Freelance	freelance.com
GMR Transcription	gmrtranscription.com
Mulberry Studio	mulberrystudio.com
Net Transcripts	nettranscripts.com
ODesk	odesk.com
Quicktate	quicktate.com
Scribie	scribie.com
TigerFish	tigerfish.com
Transcription Divas	transcriptiondivas.com
True Scribe	truescribe.net

Ubiqus	ubiqus.com
Verbal Ink	verbalink.com
Virtual Bee	workers.virtualbee.com
VOBA -oversees company looking for English speaking workers	voba.co.uk
Xerox Virtual Workforce Program	Xerox.com

23

Audio Transcriber

EMPLOYMENT STATUS Independent Contractor

EXPERIENCE REQUIRED Some/Many Opportunities for Entry Level Work

OVERVIEW

Audio transcribers listen to audio files and input the data that they hear. This is a good way to earn extra money but it's not as easy as it sounds and it's definitely not for everyone. Doing this type of work requires focus, concentration and lots and lots of patience.

Tasks may involve listening to and transcribing:

- Personal conversations
- Court hearings
- Lectures
- Business Meetings

Some companies may require experience but many hire entry level workers if you can pass their test and meet other certain requirements. For example, some companies may require you to sign a Confidentiality Agreement in order to transcribe confidential files, consent to a background check or purchase special equipment.

TIP

If you find that you like doing this type of work, you will find that there are plenty of opportunities to earn money. There are many people that make a good living as transcribers.

WORK SCHEDULE

Just as doing data entry work, you have the freedom to choose which projects you want to work and when you want to work them. The more you work, the more you earn.

WHAT YOU CAN EXPECT TO EARN

Transcribers are paid per audio file. The rate you are paid is based on the complexity of the recording. A file can be a short as 25 seconds or as long as 3- hours. The average rate of pay ranges between $3 - $20 dollars per audio file for beginners and as much as $60-$75 for experienced transcribers.

EXAMPLES:

Transcribe and review audio file - length 19 minutes and 45 seconds. Pay rate-$4.58.

Transcribe and review audio file -length 1 hour and 25 minutes. Pay rate-$25.53.

Transcribe and review audio file -length 44 minutes and 52. Pay rate-$12.11.

PAY STRUCTURE

Pay methods vary. Most companies pay via PayPal or offer direct deposit. Several companies pay weekly, others pay twice a month.

DRAWBACKS

1. The work can be boring and monotonous.
2. Some companies may offer very low fees for the work.
3. You might be required to purchase equipment for some of the higher payer jobs.

REQUIREMENTS TO GET STARTED

✓ Type at least 60 wpm with accuracy
✓ Have access to a computer with internet
✓ Good listening skills
✓ Good grammar and punctuation skills
✓ Headphone

FINDING OPPORTUNITIES

Most companies post openings on their websites. You can also find opportunities by signing up to receive job notifications from **FindTranscriptionwork.com**

Or by visiting any of the following forums or job boards:

a. **Transcription Essentials**
b. **Transcription Haven**

 *A WORD OF CAUTION*

See Chapter 22.

KEYWORD SEARCH

For best search results, enter any of the following keywords:

- General Audio Transcriber Jobs
- Audio Transcription Work
- Work From Home General Audio Transcribers Jobs
- Freelance Audio Transcription Jobs
- General Transcription Jobs from Home No Experience
- Beginners Transcription Jobs

Table 23-1 Audio Transcription Opportunities

1888typeitup.com	1888typeitup.com
3Play Media	3playmedia.com
Accutran Global	accutranglobal.com
Amazon Turk	mturk.com
Appenscribe	appenonline.appen.com
Audio File Solution	audiofilesolutions.com
Bam Transcription	bamtranscription.com
Cambridge Transcription	ctran.com/employment
Cyberdictate	cyberdictate.com
Dion Data Solutions	diondatasolutions.net
Get Transcribed	gettranscribed.com
GMR Transcription	gmrtranscription.com
Mulberry Studio	mulberrystudio.com
Net Transcripts	nettranscripts.com
ODesk	odesk.com
Quicktate	quicktate.com
Rev	rev.com/freelancers
Scribie	scribie.com
Speechpad	speechpad.com
TigerFish	tigerfish.com
Terescription	terescription.com
Transcribeme	transcribeme.com
Transcription Divas	transcriptiondivas.com
TSI	tsitranscripts.com
Verbal Ink	verbalink.com

Figure 23-1 Sample Instructions for Audio Transcription Qualification Test

This is a verbatim transcription, in which every utterance should be recorded.

1.This is a VERBATIM transcription. Include every spoken word and sound, **including um's and ah's** and stutters.

2.Use '-' for incomplete words, and ',' for stutters: wh-, what, what the . . . ?

3.Phrases like *you know, like, um,* and *ah,* should always be set off by, uh, like, commas.

4.Use Q: for the interviewer, and A: for the interviewee. If there is more than one interviewee, use B:, C:, D:, etc.

5.Punctuation and capitalization are important. Use standard punctuation as much as possible.

6.Capitalize the beginning of each speaker's statement, unless it's a clear continuation of the previous. Punctuate the end.

7.Use ',' to indicate short pauses; ' . . . ' for pauses longer than 3 seconds; [pause] for silences longer than 10 seconds.

8.Always use OK instead of ok, okay or O.K.. Also use M'kay, and 'K, where appropriate

9.If a word or phrase can't be understood, insert [??].

10.If something can't be understood because of simultaneous speakers, use . . . [SS] . . .

11.Use [SP] to indicate a word, place, or name that you are not sure how to spell. Use [SP] only after the first occurrence of the unknown word. Punctuation should follow [SP].

Taken from Speechink.com

NOTES

24

Online Mock Juror

EMPLOYMENT STATUS Independent Contractor

EXPERIENCE REQUIRED None

OVERVIEW

Online mock jurors (also called virtual jurors) are paid to serve on online mock trials. The verdicts help lawyers determine how they should best handle their arguments to win their case.

If you enjoy watching TV dramas, then you will enjoy serving as an online mock juror. It's by far an interesting way to earn extra money. The work involves reading real life case files, answering questions and submitting your verdict online.

WORK SCHEDULE

You have the flexibility to choose the hours and cases you want to work. The work setting varies from company to company. Some send out written case summaries for selected jurors to review. Others use virtual courtrooms with chat capability for attorneys to present their cases online to the jurors at a specified time and others have the jurors to listen to a recording or view a presentation of the case.

WHAT YOU CAN EXPECT TO EARN

The amount you are paid is determined by the amount of time it takes to review a case. Typical cases pay $10 to $60 per case. A case can take anywhere from 20 to 30 minutes to complete. There is no limit on the number of mock trails you can serve on.

PAY STRUCTURE

Pay methods vary. Most sites pay once a month via PayPal or mail a check.

DRAWBACKS

1. The work flow can be sporadic. There are not a lot of available online cases
2. You will need to be able to devout the right amount of time to reading the cases

REQUIREMENTS TO GET STARTED

- ✓ Be a U.S citizen
- ✓ Cannot be a convicted felon
- ✓ Cannot be under indictment for felony or misdemeanor charge
- ✓ Cannot be employed in certain parts of insurance industry
- ✓ Cannot be employed in legal profession, i.e. lawyer, legal assistant, paralegal

FINDING OPPORTUNITIES

Most companies post opening on their websites. Some run ads online

A WORD OF CAUTION

It doesn't cost anything to serve as an online mock juror. Beware of sites that ask you to send money in exchange for a list of sites that offer online jury jobs. This information can be found online for free.

KEYWORD SEARCH

For best search results, enter any of the following keywords:

- Online Mock Juror
- E-Juror Jobs
- Virtual Juror
- Online Mock Juror Jobs
- Paid Mock Juror
- Paid Jury Focus Groups
- Online Mock Jurors Needed
- Online Mock Jurors Wanted
- Online Mock Juror Sites

Table 24-1 Mock Juror Opportunities

Bryles Research	brylesresearch.com
EJury	ejury.com
Focus Forward	focusfwd.com
Jury Insights	juryinsights.com
Jury Talk	jurytalk.com
Jury Test	jurytest.com
Jury Workshop	juryworkshop.com
Jury Voice	juryvoice.com
Online Verdict	onlinverdict.com
Research Participants Institute	researchparticipant.com
Resolution Research	resolutionresearch.com
Trial Juries	trialjuries.com
Trial Practices Inc.	trialpractice.com
Virtual Jury	virtualjury.com

25

Mail Decoy Agent

EMPLOYMENT STATUS Independent Contractor

EXPERIENCE REQUIRED None

OVERVIEW

Mail decoy agents are paid to receive mail at their home addresses. This one sounds a little unbelievable but it's an actual legitimate way to earn extra money.

The work is extremely simple. It involves allowing companies to send you mailings such as catalogs, magazines, flyers and so forth. After you receive the mail, your job is to notify the mail decoy company when the mail was received and report other information. This information could include what the mail contained, the condition of the mail or other pertinent information.

The method to process the mail varies from company to company. You may have to enter the information online for one company, call an 800 for another or just mail the mailing back to others (they supply the postage).

WORK SCHEDULE

Since there isn't much work involved with this opportunity, you work at your leisure, just as long as the mail is logged in on the day that it was received. You can expect to receive approximately 15 to 30 pieces of mail in your mailbox two to three days a week. It takes about 3 minutes to process the mail.

WHAT YOU CAN EXPECT TO EARN

The amount you can expect to earn depends upon the company you sign up with and the type of mail you receive. Most companies pay a base rate per month, plus a piece rate for each mail received and processed. Pay rate range from $20 to $200 a month.

PAY STRUCTURE

Most companies pay once a month via check.

DRAWBACKS

1. Unfortunately, most companies only need one person per zip code. If they already have someone working as a mail decoy in your zip code, you may be put on a waiting list or you may not hear anything back from them
2. There are not a lot of opportunities to be a mail decoy agent because only a few companies provide this service
3. You will need to make arrangements to have the mail processed or report a break in service, if you are going to be away from home for more than a week
4. You can be disqualified from the program if you don't maintain an acceptable reporting rate.

REQUIREMENTS TO GET STARTED

- ✓ At least 18 years old
- ✓ Access to the internet
- ✓ An email address
- ✓ A mailing address
- ✓ A place to store mail for up to 6 months

FINDING OPPORTUNITIES

Most companies post opening on their websites and run ads online.

KEYWORD SEARCH

For best search results, enter any of the following keywords:

- Mail Decoy Agent
- Mail Decoy Jobs
- Mail Decoy Companies

Table 25-1 Mail Decoy Opportunities

Hauser Group	hausernet.com
Local Influencer	localinfluencer.com
Small Business Knowledge Center	sbkcenter.com
US Monitor	usmonitor.com

Super Money Tip

Double Your Earnings-
Reach Your Financial Goals Faster

I want to share with you a method I used to maximize my time and double my earnings. Mind you, this is not for everyone, especially if you are lazy at heart (no offense). But if you are ambitious, this method will help you to reach your financial goals faster with a little creative planning.

The method I am referring to is called Patch-working, pairing multiple part-time income opportunities to create a unique stream of income. In essence, it's creating multiple streams of income by doing more than one job. I know it's not rocket science or ground breaking. But what I like about most of the opportunities listed in this book is that they are flexible enough that you can fit two or more opportunities into your lifestyle without getting burdened down.

This is what I did:

1   I signed up for as many companies that I could with the following income opportunities:

- At Home Freelance Agent
- Court Researcher
- Data Entry
- Display Installer
- Drive By Inspection
- Field Audits
- Field Inspection
- Merchandising

- Micro Job Sites
- Movie Checker
- Mystery shopping (Including Video, Hospitality & Telephone)

(*You can use any ones that work best for you*)

2   I would research and apply for all of the work *from* home assignments that met the following requirements:

- In the same general area of town
- Near my home, job, church, child's school, etc.
- In the same store, mall or shopping complex
- Have the same completion dates
- Can be completed in under an hour

I call this double dipping. You will be surprised how many assignments are in the same area, neighborhood, mall or same store sometimes.

3   Then I would group the assignments by completion day and plan out my route by inputting the addresses in Google Maps or MapQuest. This would take about 40-50 minutes of planning,

For an example:

If I had 3 hours to spare on Wednesday, I would find 4-5 different jobs that I could do that were in the same general area , the same shopping complex, near my home and would net me at $150-$200 or more for the day.

Or if I planned to spend the day shopping on Saturday, I would try to find several small quick assignments I could complete while I was out shopping.

4   On the days I didn't feel like driving, I would search and apply for work *at* home small projects that I could complete in the shortest time i.e. audio transcriptions, telephone mystery shops or freelance writing projects.

Using this method, I was able to create multiple streams of income and accomplish my financial goals by working a maximum of 4.5 hours a day, 3 days a week. Once again, it's not for everyone.

ABOUT THE AUTHOR

M. Lashall Fitz is a writer and entrepreneur. She has a passion for making a difference in the lives of others. She lives in Memphis, Tennessee, enjoys connecting with nature, listening to jazz and music from the 60's.

www.ingramcontent.com/pod-product-compliance
Lightning Source LLC
Chambersburg PA
CBHW051517170526
45165CB00002B/503